Books by Frank Lebell:

HINDSIGHT

THE MANUFACTURERS' REPRESENTATIVE

PROFESSIONAL SALES REPRESENTATION

*Achieving the pinnacles of success
calls for utilizing experiences as
a succession of pitons, with each
such spike helping to secure the
rope by which the climber pulls
himself up from the earthy neces-
sities of day-to-day living into
the promising skies of the future.*

- F.L.

Professional
SALES
REPRESENTATION

A sequel to *"THE MANUFACTURERS' REPRESENTATIVE"*

by

Frank Lebell

HILLS-BAY PRESS
P.O. Box 5221
San Mateo, California 94402

Copyright © 1974 by Frank Lebell

Library of Congress
Catalog Card No. 74-80837
ISBN No. 0-9600762-2-0

First Printing August 1974
Second Printing October 1975

Published by
HILLS-BAY PRESS
P.O. Box 5221
San Mateo, California 94402

Manufactured in the United States of America

To Maryan,

with love

The chapter headed, "Must I Be The Credit Man—Too?" appeared originally in "Agent & Representative," now merged with MANA's "Agency Sales Magazine." Permission from Manufacturers' Agents National Association to reprint this and the MANA Short Form Contract is gratefully acknowledged.

— F. L.

CONTENTS

THE INTERFACE OF REPRESENTATIVE
AND SALES MANAGER

One who had read my previous book, "The Manufacturers' Representative," asked me how much time I put into research for it.

"Fifty years," I replied.

Well — trying to compress the lessons of half a century's business experience between the covers of a book led to many tough decisions about what subject matter and in-depth discussions were to be included, omitted or curtailed. Besides, as a rep writing for reps, I knew only too well the limitations of time . . . . The chapters became concise, the wording quick to the point. I was amused and quite in agreement with one reviewer who wrote of it, "Not a scholarly work but rather a seat-of-the-pants presentation."

In similar vein, "Professional Sales Representation," though complete in itself, is a follow-up of the first book. It presents new material plus, here and there, detailed extensions of several subjects previously introduced, to wind up with a potpourri of anecdotage and curiosa to browse through at coffee time.

But, aside from continuation of factual philosophy as it applies to the independent professional salesman and though primarily (but not always!) from the rep's point of view, the reader will note at times the book addresses itself directly to the marketing sales manager in the hope of clarifying various unwitting erroneous methods used in the art of dealing with reps. For example:

Where effective chemistry fails to exist between sales manager and representative, one explanation lies in the fact that all too many men become sales managers who simply do not grasp the singular nature of the kind of man drawn to manufacturers' representation, of what brought him to repping and particularly the complexities of his chosen occupation, who hold narrowly to the view that the rep is "simply a salesman." One often encounters sales managers who do not comprehend the curious, two-headed ambivalence of the manufacturers' representative, failing to realize that though the rep's primary occupation *is* selling, at the same time he functions himself as a manager, the administrative head of an enterprise.

If ever one were justified in applying the expression, "Two sides of the same coin," this is certainly it. It becomes difficult to say where the work of the one man leaves off and the other begins, as the interfacing of the sales representative with the sales manager creates a fusion of activities leading to their mutual goals. In any event, it can be assumed that what is pointed up for the one is likewise meaningful for the other. In that sense, it is hoped that not only the rep but the sales manager as well, will find in "Professional Sales Representation" helpful guideposts on the road to their mutual end goal — bigger and better sales.

— F. L.

WHAT IS A REP?

ENTREPRENEUR: "A person who organizes and manages any enterprise, especially a business, usually with considerable initiative . . ." Random *House Dictionary.* Like a manufacturers' sales representative — otherwise known as a rep — for instance?

Just what is a manufacturers' sales representative anyway? What's the attraction — is it true that a man who voluntarily chooses this occupation as a profession has to have an awful lot of guts or rocks in the head? Or, both?

Well — despite the question's facetiousness, it should be acknowledged that success in manufacturers' representation is not for the ordinary man. To begin with: it calls for carrying on in a dual role — on the one hand, representing the interests of buyers, on the other functioning in effect as the vendor. It's an occupation based, it would appear, on spending a limited number of hours making calls in solicitation of business — but that's one part of it, only the beginning:

The rep devotes time to building demand, to helping create the call-outs from the ultimate users that move merchandise off the shelves, to expediting orders, to straightening out goofs by the customer or the supplier, to acting as the factory's bill-collector, to taking customers' inventories, to checking continual changes in market conditions, to searching out new markets.

Further: to require no prodding, to be a self-starter, is a basic characteristic distinguishing the independent sales rep from the run-of-the-mill order taker. As a professional marketing authority, a consultant, the rep counsels his principals, offers suggestions for enhancing sales, for improving given products or ideas for producing new items, supplies reports direct from the field on customer reactions, on what competitors are doing. He puts on workshops, holds educational sales meetings for distributors' staffs, may even provide technical assistance for customers — countless services, all performed at his own cost.

If the man who chooses manufacturers' representation as a career is the right kind of man for it, i.e., of that limited number intended by temperament and capabilities to be "self-employed," there are rewards. A rep's life is never boring. His work takes him where the action is; he gets a broad overview and exposure to management, engineering and production in addition to marketing and sales. It's a dynamic occupation!

Modern industry is mobile, exciting, and the rep functions in the midst of hustle-and-bustle activity. Every day brings its new problems and projects to test his mettle, to stimulate by having to keep moving at the inexorable pace characteristic of business progress. And, it must be said, the financial remuneration can be very good, too — indeed, yes. But over and above the mundane, transcending all else — the rep's raison d'etre stems from a consuming desire to be his own boss. Within pragmatic limitations, manufacturers' representation offers him that opportunity, to transpose his dreams of independence into reality. The challenges are many and difficult — but the realization of achievement makes the struggle worth the while.

— F.L.

SEMANTICALLY SPEAKING

So far as this book is concerned, the abbreviation "rep" denotes individuals or firms whose occupations are commonly termed:

MANUFACTURERS' REPRESENTATIVE OR SALES REPRESENTATIVE

AGENT OR SALES AGENT

INDEPENDENT PROFESSIONAL SALESMAN

INDEPENDENT SALES CONTRACTOR

For desirable brevity and reading convenience, the sentence context will indicate by inference whether or not the word "rep" refers to a firm rather than to just one individual.

Also — the term "sales manager" as used herein, is to be understood as including "Marketing Manager" or variations of that title. There are those who look upon the manufacturer's market Planning, Development, Departmental Management and, finally, Sales Management as though each were an individual occupation in itself, despite the fact that these subjects blend into each other so that distinctions become difficult, if not unnecessary. In any event, for the purposes of this book, the reader is asked to accept the rep's point of view in that, so far as he is concerned, the manufacturer's marketing activities are embodied and personified in the Sales Manager.

— F.L.

"The road to riches is paved with good lines"

I

THE REP EVALUATES A PROSPECTIVE LINE

UNDERLYING ASPECTS OF A NEW COMMITMENT

Whenever I hear a man being complimented on having proved himself to be "a good loser," I wonder just what the hell it is that's so praiseworthy about being a loser — especially, a "good" one!

The thought hit me particularly on one occasion when a rep acquaintance was telling me about losing a line that was just beginning to bring him some return after a number of hard, preliminary months of working on it.

"I just happened to pick it up at a trade show," he said. "Got to talking with this guy at their booth. He said they didn't have a rep in my territory; looked like a pretty good line — worth a try, anyway — so I took it on, right then and there. Heck — I didn't know the company was owned by this big conglomerate, just started on doing away with independent reps in order to consolidate all their factories into one office of their own."

He laughed. "This sales manager didn't know himself that he was soon going to be out of a job! Guess it cost me a couple of grand. Oh, well — that's the way this business goes, eh?" He shrugged, and laughed again. Not that I felt he should break out in great devastating sobs, but I kept wondering what was so funny about working for months for nothing, and losing a couple of thousand dollars.

One of the debatable elements of manufacturers' representation as a profession is the generally held assumption that
sales representation agreements are *bound* to be lacking in
permanence. This is not to deny that, at one time or another,
a rep will find it necessary to relinquish custody of a line — as
in termination, perhaps resignation. One must acknowledge
that severance of an established relationship with a principal
is an ever-present hazard of sales representation, perhaps a
likelihood, even an eventuality. Nevertheless, it is entirely
possible for representatives and manufacturers to maintain
mutually profitable and satisfactory relationships down
through the many long years. If the truth be told, it is the
superficial degree of judgment exhibited by so many reps at
the very beginning in exploring and evaluating a prospective
line that has much to do with leading to short-lived representation agreements and, in turn, to the moot reputation of
instability in repping as an occupation.

Crystal balls are somewhat undependable but just a bit of
digging in the right places by the rep at the time of contemplating the representation arrangement, might conceivably
reveal aspects having much pro or con bearing on a *lasting*
relationship — nor need this take too long in most cases.
Considering the investment a rep must make in the marketing
and promotion of a new line, it would seem incumbent upon
him to search out and appraise conditions existing *other than
the obvious* before committing himself. Too few do.

As in the case of the example cited, there are those who
take on just about any and every line that becomes available
— a kind of desperate policy justified by the strained theory
that if you bet on enough horses, you'll come out ahead.
Well, true enough, the thoughtful, far-sighted rep too, bets —
BUT selectively, judiciously. He looks first at his *capital,* i.e.,
his time — bringing to bear every possible bit of judgment
before deciding whether or not an available prospective line
warrants the degree of time and, of course, the attention it
would take from his other lines. Then, once the usual *pri-*

mary elements that go to making up a "good line" are deemed present, the rep who knows his business will probe below the surface, exploring certain conditions which experience indicates will have influence on how well things may be expected to work out on that line.

Of course, the first thing that comes to mind in considering a new line is the amount of time available for arriving at a decision. Reps who should know better are nevertheless sometimes panicked into grabbing a line without giving it the exploring it should have because of fear some other rep will beat them to it. A sales manager's hasty acceptance of a rep's application for his line, based on a few favorable but superficial observations, doesn't speak well for permanence of the sales agreement either. At any rate, so far as the rep is concerned, a fairly reasonable, enlightening appraisal of a prospective new line's desirability really need take no more than an hour or two — at most, perhaps a day. In fact, just the minutes required for a few properly placed phone calls might very possibly get you a large part of the kind of information you should have.

> *A farmer sold a mule to his neighbor. About a week later, they met. The one who had bought the animal waved an irate fist in the other's face.*
>
> *"That was a dirty trick to play on a neighbor,"* he stormed. *"Selling me a blind mule! Why did you do that?"*
>
> *"I don't get it" disclaimed the other. "What makes you think he's blind?"*
>
> *"Of course he is! I hitched him up to a wagon and drove him down the road a piece. What does that blasted mule do but head for the fence, keeps going right on through it, breaks up my wagon, gets himself all scratched up and cut up, with the blood and everything, on account he couldn't see*

where he was going. Blind, I tell yuh!"

The former owner shook his head. "Naw," he said. "He ain't blind. That mule, he just don't give a damn."

That's an old story but it illustrates the kind of rep who doesn't give a damn about where he's going in this repping business because every so often one such does come along to momentarily clutter up the scenery. A newcomer to the business whom I knew for a while, before he dropped from sight, expressed his philosophy in simple terms to me one time: "I take on just about everything that becomes available and give it a try," he said. "Who can tell — it might be a sleeper. If it doesn't prove out, I simply drop it and look for something else. What's to hurt — you just have to keep trying."

Well, what's to hurt is if a man doesn't value his time any more than that, if he isn't concerned about the reputation he acquires for always offering the trade questionable products, he ought to be in some other business. And yet there are those who, if a line seems to hold any promise at all will, with the briefest consideration, sign up for it. For such reps who just don't give a damn, neither should anyone else. As competitors, they won't be much of a bother because though they're here today, they'll be gone tomorrow.

No one has that gift of prophecy which will enable him to determine beforehand, beyond doubt, that a line is going to be a desirable addition to his roster in view of the wide variations in circumstances surrounding the availability of a given line. But assume you've learned the primary require-ments of a prospective line are there — presumably saleable, attractive products, competitive pricing, satisfactory commis-sion rate, prevalence of customer good will if the line has been sold in your territory before — those easily determined factors that go toward making a "good line." You would do well then to carry on your evaluation procedures with this kind of hard-headed thinking to guide you: suppose someone you barely knew asked you to make him an *unsecured* loan of a thousand dollars or perhaps even several thousands, at what would seem to be a good rate of interest. Regardless of the attractive return indicated, you'd first want to make mighty sure this investment was going to be placed with à responsible party — wouldn't you?

In the same sense — when taking on a new line, wouldn't you have to make a very real dollars-and-cents investment in this new principal's operations? You don't go out promoting a line without the procedure costing you money, do you? Naturally! but — your judgment can be no better than the facts in hand. In consequence, at the very beginning, make determination of the manufacturer's financial condition, that most important requirement which is so often given only a "lightly once over" despite having so much bearing on one's future with that line. Is he financially able to promote, to advertise, to meet tough conditions, to pay his rep commissions on time, to make operational loans from normal sources as needed, to finance new products, to weather periods when business drops off, to withstand the effects of a serious strike? For reasonably applicable answers, don't just accept the sales manager's off-hand assurances that this company is financially sound. (It is even possible, he might not know himself!) If the company is not closely held (as it might be in a one-owner or in a family business) and assuming it is "public," begin by consulting the very informative data on the corporation readily available at your securities broker. You'll find it *most* revealing.

If you don't already have acquaintance with a securities broker, look ahead — make it your business to set up a relationship by buying some stock. (If nothing else, as I mentioned previously in "The Manufactures' Representative," it is good business anyway to own some stock in your principals' companies, if only a few shares, regardless of what you do in the way of trading on the stock market otherwise. Aside from that, in all fairness, you should make yourself a client if you are going to use the stock broker's services).

The broker can supply his customers immediately with extremely detailed information on any of the companies listed on the stock exchanges. Aside from his people's own research, he will have on hand such data as that given in the Standard & Poor poop sheets which set out a given subject company's fundamental position in its industry with authoritative, meaningful statistics such as financial statements. Profit and loss figures for a good many years back are given as well as dividends paid, kind of market or trade or products wherein the company is strong, big contracts perhaps recently received or likely, in some cases specific reasons for certain major developments that might be expected in the future, and so on — a concentrated compilation of pertinent data of the kind a prospective investor would want to know, right at his fingertips. This highly applicable information, so potentially significant in evaluating the company, is yours for the asking, *in moments,* simply by request from your broker.

(Incidentally, although this of course will take longer, ask the prospective principal for a copy of their current year's report to stockholders. Lots of fascinating and fairly reliable information is contained in these fancy brochures. If you own shares in your principals' companies, you receive these automatically. It's quite illuminating to compare them — especially the figures — with the less formal reports of what those companies are doing!).

Note, too, that even though you are in a city distant from home, but are negotiating for a line (as, perhaps, at a trade show), the major brokers have offices in many of the country's main cities so that, even under those conditions, you will find it feasible to get fast information from the broker with whom you ordinarily deal. Also, though the company in which you are interested is not one which is ordinarily "traded," your broker might come up with some applicable information about them anyway, through the split second electronic communication they have with their information sources.

With this kind of data before you, plus your talks with the sales manager, determine for yourself: has the company been making progress over the years? Growing or retrogressing? So-so? If the manufacturer hasn't shown a great deal of progress — just gives out with an airy "next year" prediction for disa or data plan — is there a good explanation? Could it be the incompetence of their marketing methods or their sales management? Are they under-capitalized? Not sufficiently experienced in their chosen field? Products becoming outdated? Legal procedures in progress with possible dire consequences?

Suppose, for one reason or another, you can't get the desired information from a stock broker as, for example, in cases where the company is not "public." Well, you can still learn lots about them, simply by consulting your bank and asking that the company be checked out. This is best done by contacting the manager of your bank or, if not him, at least some upper echelon officer. Tell him just what you want to know — the financial status of the company, past and present, what may be known about its management personnel, its ownership, and any past history available. Who knows better how to dig up this kind of information? In all probability, the bank will come up with a raft of valuable information for you. Again — with today's communication methods, if the bank doesn't have the info on tap, they can get it for you very quickly.

Even so far, it's possible you may already begin to see rocks showing up that could wreck a lengthy, satisfactory relationship with this company. However, we'll assume all looks AOK — so far.

The catalog

A most significant element in adjudication of a line's worth is the manufacturer's catalog! This is the rep's third basic tool — just as mandatory as his car and his telephone, if not more so! The requirements in a manufacturer's literature will vary from one industry to another but some basics are common to all. Study your prospective principal's catalog closely. Does the wording give the customer appropriate descriptions or is it mainly blurb stuff? How about applicable details — clear pictures or understandable line drawings where called for in technical products, weight, dimensions, colors, material, appearance, compliance with safety and legal conditions — namely, those more *common* factors with which the customer is concerned and which are bound to come up when talking with him? Just how *informative* is it?

The detailed makeup of a catalog is not for us to get into here but, since you must know what a *good* catalog should be like, it is only necessary to remember there is something radically wrong or at least suspiciously strange when a manufacturer does not have ready for distribution a comprehensive, clearly worded, attractive catalog, along with understandable direction manuals where called for, as well as other likely literature pertaining to his products. Look with a jaundiced eye upon the sales manager who brushes off lack of literature with some remark like, "We're working on it." Nine times out of ten, that's simply evasion. If you're being asked to work with a manufacturer who's apathetic about supplying literature describing his products, who doesn't realize the importance of having a good catalog or who isn't financially able to pay for an attractive, informative catalog, you'd better know it right in the beginning and, unless the circumstances are very unusual, you'd do best to pass that line up.

The sale manager

The sales manager who interviews you presumably will determine the long or short of your tenure with his company if you become their rep. Use all your skill, every bit of understanding you have of human nature to size up this guy. Don't hesitate to ask leading, searching questions. If the prospective principal is a large company, try to learn: is he a *real* "head man" or only a figurehead? Does he have clout or must he defer to a superior for carrying on his relationships with the reps and the trade? Does he seem to know his business and, if not, does he know *that* — and is he willing to be helped?

Use your own approach and wording, of course, as befits your personality, but make your queries very clear. Ask, "What were your gross sales for the past three years and what kind of profits were made?" (Compare what *he* tells you to information secured from the previously described sources!) If no money was made — why? (Would you want to tie in with a loser?) What is definitely in the works in the way of promotions, advertising programs, new products? Do his answers sound as though all the load will be on the reps? What may be expected from the factory in the way of *realistic* sales help? Don't just accept his grandly voiced, "We cooperate with our reps" — pin him down with, "Specifically, how? *What* do you do?"

The manner in which Mr. Sales Manager responds to plain spoken questions will tell you much about whether or not you ought to take that line on. If he's frank, you have something to talk about. If he's evasive or, worse yet, *resents* your questioning, bristles because you want to know just what kind of an outfit this is before you tie in with it, I'd be awfully skeptical about his line. If he doesn't accept the fact that your time, money and intensive effort will be invested in any line you take on, that you have your reputation to protect, you have a pretty good idea of what your future relationship with the man would be.

If, after your preliminary contacts and interview, you're still on talking terms, keep doing just exactly that — talking as long as time permits. Take him to lunch — maybe he's the kind whose tongue loosens up with a couple of drinks in him. Better yet — take him out in the evening for dinner. He'll have more time, be more relaxed, and consequently be more talkative. The more he talks, the more you'll learn about what you're getting into — and you can keep on making points for yourself, as the ball keeps rolling.

By the way — as a footnote to the "couple of drinks": does he confine himself to a normal one or two sociable drinks? Or, do you see signs of the excessive drinker, of whom there seem to be so many nowadays — men who hurt not only themselves and their families, but others who have to depend on them? I recall being afflicted with a sales manager who was always "out in the field," travelling from territory to territory, ostensibly working. In actual fact, he was using such trips only to get away from his home city, so that he could go on prolonged drunken sprees. All he did when he was in my territory was waste my time trying to keep him out of trouble. It's a sad fact but with alcoholism so widespread, getting loaded down (sic!) with one such is always a likely possibility.

Another kind that comes along once in a while, not too dissimilar, using "field trips" for purposes other than business, is the sales manager who, though perhaps a married man, has arrived at the years of indiscretion, and looks to his reps to provide feminine companionship for him when he comes to town. He shows up with a desire to gambol in fresh, green pastures, subject usually to the tradition of men's preference for blonde fields when it comes to gamboling. This is no place for moralizing but is simply to point up the desirability, if possible, of learning beforehand whether or not you are going to be expected to be the purveyor of acreage for a frisky-minded sales manager to prance around in. It can happen — and does.

This writer still winces at the memory of a regional sales manager visiting my territory, presumably in the interests of a very important line I was repping, who took considerable umbrage because I was unable to come up with "a little black book" of phone numbers for him, and afterwards made every effort to have me fired. This kind of thing comes to a matter of principles between the sales manager and the rep, but it is one of the finer points to anticipate if you possibly can in view of its potentialities for trouble. Unless, that is — uh — well — hmmmmm . . . .

As I write, I can just hear some rep snorting, "Hell's fire, by the time I'd go through all that investigating stuff, somebody else would have grabbed the line." Well, yes — could be. Impelled by the high octane of wishful thinking for fuel, there are those reps who race to the finish line of decision. But for the fellow who "grabbed" without making all the enquiries possible about the line in question, all one can say is, "lotsa luck — and why don't you try the slot machines? You'll get faster action for your results."

As a matter of fact, making the described enquiries need not take longer than, at worst, overnight (unless, of course, you're stymied by its being Saturday or Sunday, as when you might be in negotiation at a trade show. In that case, if you can't stall things along until Monday, of course you're just going to have to do the best you can. There are times — bound to be — when you will have to grit your teeth and take the plunge because the line looks very attractive on the surface and the circumstances compel you to give with a "Yes" or "No" immediately. So, if it's "Yes," you make with a little prayer and hope you've lived right).

Before going on, let's discuss this "time" thing a bit more. Though you may have only an hour or two within which to make up your mind, you can still learn considerable even in that limited period about the prospective principal, by means already described. But, in addition, and even on a weekend, if, as is so likely, your deal is in prospect at a convention or trade show, there are the other of the company's reps whom you can consult. Try to get one or two aside in confidential conversation and pump for all the information you can possibly extract about the prospective principal.

Under some circumstances, depending on the day or hour, if you are friendly with one of their reps located in another territory, give him a fast phone call. A couple of bucks for a toll call might pay off handsomely in producing some interesting information. You might ask for comments on the manufacturer's productivity skills, whether or not the management employs sound, progressive marketing procedures. Since you are in an entirely different territory and, being on the same side! other reps are not likely to be afraid to tell you the facts, at least from their point of view. (I've never known a *real* rep who wasn't always ready to give you his opinion — on anything!)

Along the same lines, try to strike up a conversation with the company's assistant personnel — especially men who work close to the sales manager, as "assistant" or "regional" sales managers. You can almost bet that they are going to want to impress you with their importance and consequently are likely to give you some intriguing dope about the boss man and the company. Could be very valuable sources of information.

Of course, how much weight you give to these various sources is going to have to be up to your judgment. No one can do that for you.

A common time-tight situation is the one when a sales manager comes into town and you receive a phone call from him, wherein he tells you he's in town for a short time and that his company is looking for a new rep. He gives you a few words of description about his line, you express interest, and he then asks you to come over to the hotel to talk it over.

If the company is "public," even before you get together with him at his hotel, look to the information on one of those poop sheets at your broker's and you come into the interview already armed with some very important factual material about the company! If there isn't enough time before the interview, drop in or phone your broker's office right after you leave the hotel and get whatever data he has describing the company and its operations. If the company isn't "public," as described before, have your bank check them out for you.

Now, even though the sales manager was interested in you, in all probability he had made appointments with other prospective reps and so he asked you to sit tight until the following day, when he would get in touch with you. Don't sit on your hands. Act! Armed with the data from your broker or bank, *you* phone *him* first thing in the following morning — with tact and discretion, of course — but concoct some question out of what you've learned about the company as an excuse for your call. Don't wait for him to call you; he might not! Your showing of great interest, your fast action on-the-ball kind of follow-up should impress him and help that much in your favor — *if* you really *are* interested in the line.

Which brings us to the point that, despite its self-evidence, strangely enough is so often overlooked by reps, namely: IT IS JUST AS IMPORTANT TO THE SALES MANAGER TO HAVE GOOD REPRESENTATIVES AS IT IS FOR THE REP TO ACQUIRE A GOOD ROSTER OF LINES. HE NEEDS YOU AS WELL AS YOU NEED HIM. IT'S A TWO-WAY STREET! □

II

SALES AGREEMENTS

SOME OF THE PITFALLS AND SUCH — EN GARDE!

*ANY SO-CALLED MANUFACTURERS' REP-
RESENTATIVE WHO ENTERS INTO A SALES
REPRESENTATIVE AGREEMENT WITHOUT A
WRITTEN CONTRACT IS ONE WHO WOULD
GO UP IN A BALLOON WITHOUT BALLAST!
SUCH A TRUSTING SOUL MIGHT JUST AS
WELL STOP WASTING TIME READING THIS
BOOK BECAUSE, WITH THAT UNPRAGMATIC
OUTLOOK, HE ISN'T GOING TO LAST IN THE
REP BUSINESS LONG ENOUGH TO USE WHAT
HE READS HEREIN.*

By way of contract form, the experience consensus of the better trade associations is available, such as exampled by the Electronic Representatives Association report on the detailed provisions of a properly constituted sales agreement. (Reproduced in Chapter XIV of "The Manufacturers' Representative"). The MANA "short form" contract, which has been widely used for many years, is probably adequate for most arrangements. (That one is reproduced at the end of this chapter.)

The referenced forms need not be followed word for word (as a quick example: there are those who believe the word "representative" should be used rather than "agent"). Their provisions depend on the individual circumstances but they

present in concise form the requirements of a sales representation agreement. Also, an agreement form which every rep
would do well to have readily at hand, offering twelve pages
of varying provisions to cover almost any kind of contin-
gency, can be obtained from MANA* by request, at no
charge, and there are other associations who provide model
sales agreements embodying the essence of long years of
experience. But, no matter who composes the contract or
how it sounds to you, you will do well to have your attorney
look it over.

Try to roll your own.

Many manufacturers don't use ready-made contract forms
of their own, but have them drawn up as the need arises. It is
a good idea and preferable to have a "standard" form of your
own on tap, always ready to produce as soon as expedient
during the negotiations. It would presumably have included
all the provisions you want, especially reasonable termination
conditions, and could help forestall prolonged discussions of
points which, in the final analysis, would probably be acceptable to the principal anyway.

Split commissions

Since the situation doesn't arise in all industries, this point
is sometimes overlooked but in cases where orders may be
worked up in one area but are formally placed from another
territory, the contract should have definite "split commission" provisions spelled out, i.e., to specify what percentage
of the commission goes to each of the two or perhaps three
reps concerned. In some cases, which rep has done the major
portion of building up a big order or just where the work of
one rep leaves off and another begins, can be difficult to
determine, leaving lots of room for dispute. If such a situa-

---

* MANA (Manufacturers' Agents National Association),
  3130 Wilshire Blvd., Los Angeles, California 90010

tion has not been anticipated in the sales agreement, there can be only one answer to this possibility: the principal's decision will have to be invoked and accepted as final, it being assumed he would want to take care of each of his reps as fairly as he would know how.

The cause for exclusive sales rights

Make absolutely sure your territory and selling rights are clearly defined, these being often the direct causes of contract termination. It is especially important to establish unequivocally that you have exclusive selling rights *to all the manufacturers' products* in the stated territory but, *if* there are to be exceptions, such as on certain models, perhaps on "house accounts" or some other of this manufacturers' operations, and *if* you agree, these should be specifically written out.

In a lawsuit stemming from the case of a manufacturer using a flimsy excuse to get rid of a rep so that he could avoid paying the commission due on a big order, the court held in favor of the rep. The reasoning: that when evidence establishes a contract has been terminated in part by attempting to escape payment of a commission, it infers the termination was in bad faith. Though the order had been placed by the customer directly with the factory, the fact that the contract called for exclusive sales rights in the territory, *made it unnecessary to prove that the rep had taken the actual order himself.*

An acquaintance of mine was telling me recently about being confronted with an old, disreputable practice which, evidently, still crops up in some industries. It seems he had discovered that he had a double-dealing principal who had developed a series of products practically duplicating his standard line though of cheaper materials, but under a different brand name, and selling in this rep's territory at prices slightly below the original line, *without* any commissions to the rep.

In such a situation, while none are ideal, you have three possible ways to go. Put it to the manufacturer that, under the circumstances, he can have no objections if you take on a line produced by another manufacturer which is competitive to his. In all fairness, why not — isn't he giving you competition? Or, propose that he appoint you to sell his *secondary* line as well as the original line — at a fitting commission rate — leaving it to your judgment where and when to offer for sale one series or the other, perhaps both.

The third and of course probably most tempting course to follow would be to plan dropping the line altogether and replacing it with another one manufactured by fair-minded people — admittedly not an easy thing to do.

The reason I bring up that unpleasant and inconclusive incident here is only to point up the fallacy of omitting coverage of "exclusive selling rights" when signing up a representation agreement. That rep, you can be sure, was not engaged in the electronic industry or he would not have allowed himself to be made the victim of such a dilemma. It being known this writer spent many years in the electronic industry, I may well be charged with chauvinism in making such an allusion but, from what I have seen of other industries, especially those long established, travelling in deep, well-worn ruts, I respectfully suggest there are some things which can be learned from the electronic industry. For example:

To an electronic rep, it would be surprising to find that the question of "exclusive selling rights" comes up at all. In that industry, "exclusive" is all but taken for granted except that, as a formality, the point is always covered in writing in the sales contract. No electronic rep takes on a line without including rights to sell all of the manufacturer's products, unless specific exceptional conditions exist and which are plainly brought out and agreed upon *at the time of negotiating the sales contract.* Such a case might be that of a manufacturer producing widely diversified series of products, their appeal being to varied markets. Since reps are pretty apt to confine their activities to prescribed fields, the manufacturer might feel he should divide his products among two or even more reps in the same territory. That would have some drawbacks (customer confusion as to just who reps the products in which he is interested) but could be acceptable because the product categories would not be competitive.

Competing with an ex-principal

This has been pointed out before but because it should be an absolute non-non! it is emphasized here: that is, the case of your prospective principal wanting to include a clause to the effect that if your relationship is severed, you will not enter into the sale of competitive products thereafter for some lengthy period of time. Horse-bleep! No-no! Out! There are reps who stupidly acquiesce to this murderous condition but you can squelch any dispute on the point by letting this manufacturer know he's spitting in the breeze because the courts have held no agreement is valid which prevents a man from earning an honest living!

Product liability

Man, oh man — give this your best thought! Include an iron-clad clause in your contract placing responsibility for product performance, warranties, guarantees, patent infringement, bodily injury etc., etc. directly on the manufacturer. But better yet: take out product liability insurance, regardless of what it says in your contract! Check this out with your insurance man and attorney. (Your trade association may already have or can arrange for low-cost group liability insurance for its members.) Such protection is fully as important as auto insurance — your only *real* protection in view of the product liability suits coming up in the tens of thousands per year, particularly prompted by the recent passage of special Consumer Protection legislation.

Don't be misled into thinking that because you have noth-

ing to do with the product's makeup and have no control over its production or use, that you're not responsible. The courts have held that reps who make the sale are "in the line of distribution" and, under some circumstances, may have to share responsibility. (See the chapter headed, "Agent vs. Representative" for further discussion of this responsibility subject.)

The rep as a sucker

It is possible for unwitting reps to fall prey to manipulations permitting manufacturers to take unfair advantage of them, sometimes to the extent of innocently becoming involved in sharp practices, approaching even illegality. One of the methods used by unscrupulous manufacturers to dupe reps is so common that the rep can blame only himself for allowing himself to be victimized:

This is the kind of situation that comes about when the rep takes on a line without having checked with the previous rep as to why there was a representation termination. Had he done so, he might have learned that the previous rep gave the line up because he grew tired of waiting for long overdue commissions, that the rep before him likewise quit for the same reason and that, ridiculous though it may seem, a number of reps could have had the same line in the same territory, worked it for only some months, and then dropped it because they couldn't collect their commissions. I know of one case where five reps had the same line in succession within two years (four besides the writer!). The reason the rep takes the licking in such cases is because the total amount of commissions due him amounts to only a few hundred dollars, obviously too small for hiring collections agencies and attorneys, so he just cusses the "manufacturer" out and leaves the cheater to go on taking advantage of other reps.

That unpleasant experience happens very frequently to those new to repping, as I was at that time. Nowadays, in some industries, the main office of one's trade association very likely has set up machinery for acting on these situations. Though perhaps too much for an individual rep, if your association hasn't already done so, it is entirely practical and not too expensive to make an arrangement at group rates with a national credit agency to handle such collections if, so and when called for, resulting in minimum cost to the individual members. And, there are ways to guard against getting involved with impecunious, misrepresenting or chiseling operators in the first place, as indicated in the previous chapter.

Sometimes an overbearing manufacturer's callous lack of consideration for the rep leads him into procedures that may be illegal. As an instance, you have the manufacturer willing to quote a special low price because a prospective customer is talking big quantities. In order to get that price down as far as possible, he is likely to arbitrarily cut the rep's commission accordingly. While it isn't fair, but having no other choice, the rep himself may agree to the smaller commission rate, consoling himself with the thought of the large orders looming up. BUT — one should make sure that the *same low pricing* is available to *all* avenues of trade of a similar class.* Otherwise, Federal laws may be violated and the fact of the rep accepting the principal's dictum might in all innocence get *him* embroiled if the manufacturer wasn't aware of or chose to disregard the legalities involved. It's bad enough to take a cut in your commission rate but make sure you're not going to be entangled in some possible illegality.

A sad story from my early experience was taking on a new line just as the principal became engaged in a price war with a competitor. Knowing nothing yet of the battling, I went out taking orders according to the price list with which I had been supplied — only to have it announced less than a week

---

* Same thing applies to advertising allowances — or any similar concessions.

later, before the orders were even received, that some of the items on the list had been reduced. While I was busily engaged trying to explain *that* away, came still another price drop, announced in wires to the trade, my principal telling me nothing directly; I had to learn it from the customers! At that point, I telegraphed my resignation!

Well, that kind of situation is a bit unusual but it was graphic exemplification, in taking on a new line, of the need for the rep to have a clear-cut understanding on pricing. He should know whether or not the price list supplied is firm or subject to "negotiation" under some conditions, whether or not there will be customer price protection in the event of a change, and, very important, that the principal have understanding of the Robison-Patman Act and complies with it because, in commercial practices, it is all too easy for the ignorant to violate that law.

Another kind of mess not too infrequent, about which I also had to learn the hard way, was in the case of taking on a one-instrument line which, listing at $150, sold to the distributor at 60% off or $60.00 net. When my sample arrived, I was taken aback by the fact that it had been shipped not only C.O.D. and at the customer's price but via air at that — so that I had to come up with $78.00. Well, I paid it! I was still trying to build up a good roster of lines, I was anxious to get out with the demonstrator and start taking orders. I felt that a simple letter to the sales manager would take care of the situation . . . .

I wrote that letter — it went unanswered. I mailed two follow-ups, with still no response. In the meantime, I had been writing orders because the product was one of a kind then in short supply, and getting business on it was easy. But deliveries weren't coming through. I phoned the sales manager to expedite the orders, also bringing up the subject of the "collect" sample. He assured me most vehemently that he would take care of everything, that they had been so awfully busy — etc., etc.

Finally, the orders began to arrive. Many of the devices failed to function properly right from the start. Customers returned them — and heard nothing further from the factory, despite *their* follow-ups. I received nothing — no invoices, no refund on the sample (which had developed a defect), no commission checks, no nothing. I tried to call — to learn the company's phone service had been disconnected. In only a few months from the time this "manufacturer" started, they went into bankruptcy.

How would I handle the same situation, were it to occur today? In the first place, I wouldn't! It just wouldn't happen. That is, if the line interested me, at the start of negotiations I would have investigated the factory's background, starting with its financial status and, the product being an intricate electrical instrument, I would have particularly checked their engineering qualifications and facilities. In a case like the one described, everything would have come to a complete stop right then and there, so far as I was concerned.

As for a sample shipped to a rep "collect," and at customer prices at that — I would have greeted such a strange procedure with refusing to accept the shipment, and would have put in a phone call immediately requesting an explanation. If a proper explanation were not forthcoming, I would simply instruct the carrier to return the shipment to the shipper — "collect" for all costs. I wouldn't bother writing letters because I would want to know *right now* whether the "sample collect" was only a clerical error; if policy, they would have my resignation as fast as I could get it to them.

I heard one time of an irate rep who settled scores rather ironically with a manufacturer giving him the run-around insofar as commissions were concerned. The rep had received a letter terminating his sales agreement, accompanied by the demand that he return the quite valuable samples in his possession. His two or three successive requests for commissions due him were ignored. Instead, he received a sternly worded wire demanding that he'd better ship the samples back immediately — or else! — although it allowed they could be sent "collect" (meaning, of course, the manufacturer was willing to pay the freight). Whereupon, the rep did send the samples back but "misunderstood" (?) the instructions to ship "collect." He shipped "C.O.D." — the amount called for including the commissions due him. It worked! He got his money!

Every rep in the business who has been at it for some time, can relate his share of horrendous stories, of having been victimized by chicanery or his own youthful naivete and inexperience. But aside from unscrupulous manufacturers, it is quite possible and it sometimes happens that conscientious, entirely well intentioned principals fail in their efforts, being undercapitalized, inexperienced, unable to meet competition or whatever, in turn causing their reps unanticipated losses. One can only repeat and emphasize the Better Business Bureau's admonishment, "Investigate before you invest."* For applications of this great slogan to repping, refer to the line evaluation suggestions set out in Chapter I.

Contracts with your salesmen

The practice of making up a written contract between the rep employer and the salesman he hires is growing among the more thoughtful and experienced reps. The document should be drawn up by an attorney although your trade association may be able to supply you with guiding forms. Most of the provisions to be incorporated are pretty much self evident, such as setting out duties, working periods, holiday and vacation observances, expenses allowed and refundable, bene-

---

* Remember Ed Wynn's invention of the eleven-foot pole — for people he wouldn't touch with a ten-foot pole?

fits such as insurance and pensions, ownership shares in your corporation and so on.

However, it is just because such conditions are so commonplace and readily taken for granted that misunderstandings and disputes may arise if not written out in detail. For example, the automobile: who supplies it? If it is a car that has seen much use, who pays for its parts replacements, for tires, batteries, and miscellaneous repairs, as well as gas and oil? The liability insurance, if the salesman supplies his own car, should include the employer among "the insured" as well as the car's owner — the policy to incorporate this. (Ordinarily, the premium won't be any higher).

You might keep a couple of other significant points in mind when drawing up the contract with your men:

If they are on commission and divisions are established between your salesmen according to brand lines or perhaps sub-territories, specify how the commission is to be split or who gets the commission in the event any orders come in from one man's jurisdiction which, according to your arrangement with them would ordinarily be due to the other.

Ironically enough, termination can be as much a toughie when you sever relationships with one of your salesmen, as occurs when you and a manufacturer part company, the shoe now being on the other foot! The potentialities make it necessary that the contract spell out in anticipation of such items, as that, upon leaving you, the salesman is to relinquish any lists of customers and prospects called on, along with the names of all individuals involved in the customers' managements, engineering and purchasing departments, that he is to return all catalogs, samples, sales books, credit cards, dictating equipment, tools, etc., etc.

Include a "thereafter" provision. That is (unless he's been on straight salary) specify how much, at what rate and period of time, as well as on which business the salesman will receive remuneration after termination (*if any!*).

While I firmly believe the prudent businessman will take up anything in the way of a contract with his attorney, and the foregoing no less, there are two especially serious points which are probably of the greatest consequence when dispensing with an employee's services, on which legal advice is most important, namely:

1) The erstwhile salesman becomes a rep or employee for one of your principals. (I'm sure you don't need pictures on this one! Who isn't familiar with the ever-present hazard of repping, that of one's salesman departing and taking along with him one or two of your lines?)

2) What about the salesman agreeing not to call on your customers for a period of one year with products which could be substituted for those brands which he was selling for you while in your employ? Actually, in what way would this be different from the attempts of one of your principals trying to keep *you* from taking on a competitive line after severance of relations with him?

Talk it over with your attorney!

What it comes to is that in putting together a contract of this kind *you* are in effect acting like the manufacturer who has you sign up a representation agreement with him so that, generally, the points covered in that contract are probably largely applicable when you, in turn, sign up a salesman to enter your employ — one of those changes of pace (face?) that makes manufacturers' representation such a "different" occupation.   □

A Short Form of Agency Agreement

MANA Short Contract

This Agreement by and between ...., known as the Company, and ...., known as the Manufacturers' Agent; in accordance with and subject to, the following:

1. The products which the Manufacturers' Agent is authorized to sell, and the prices and terms, are as shown on the addenda to this Agreement, or as specified in subsequent price books, bulletins, and other authorized documents.

2. The prices of sale, at which the Manufacturers' Agent is to sell such products, shall be those currently in effect and established from time to time in the Company's price books, bulletins and in other authorized releases.

3. Said Manufacturers' Agent further agrees to abide and comply with all sales policy and operating regulations of the Company, as issued from time to time and will not obligate or contract in behalf of the Company without first having received written authority to do so from an Executive of the Company.

4. The territory in which the Manufacturers' Agent is to work is as follows: ....
....
This territory is exclusive unless otherwise stated in writing. The Manufacturers' Agent shall be credited with all orders accepted by the Company from this territory, as long as this Agreement remains in force.

5. Commissions due to the Manufacturers' Agent shall be payable before the 15th day of the month following (date of shipment by the Company) OR (date of payment by the purchaser) OR (date of acceptance by the Company). If orders are returned to and accepted by the Company for credit, commissions paid or credited to the Manufacturers' Agent for such orders shall be deducted from the amount of other commissions due to the Manufacturers' Agent, if that amount is sufficient; otherwise, commissions paid on such returned-for-credit orders shall be refunded to the Company by the Manufacturers' Agent within 30 days of written request by the Company.

6. The Company reserves the right at all times to reject any and all orders because of unsatisfactory credit rating of the purchaser. On sales of unrated new accounts, the Manufacturers' Agent may be required to furnish local credit information and submit full information with orders. The Manufacturers' Agent will also assist in the collection of past due accounts owing the Company by customers located in said Manufacturers' Agent's territory.

7. When an order originates in one agent's territory for shipment into another agent's territory, or in any case when the commission is divided between two or more of the Company's agents, the commission shall be divided according to the schedule shown on the addendum to this Contract, with no part of the commission being retained by the Company.

8. During the first year, this Agreement may be terminated for any reason by either party upon 30 days' notice to the other by registered mail. After this Agreement has been in force for one full year, it may be terminated by either party for any reason upon six months' notice to the other by registered mail. The Manufacturers' Agent shall be paid commissions on all orders from his territory accepted by the Company prior to the effective termination date, even though such orders may be shipped or paid for after the effective termination date.

COMPANY APPROVAL:

By ....

Signature

....

Title

....

Date

....

Manufacturers' Agent

III

TERMINATIONS — INEVITABLE?

The sales manager giveth; the sales manager taketh away. All hail, Caesar!

When a rep enters into an agreement to represent a given manufacturer, it certainly isn't very good psychology to dwell on the defeatist likelihood of the agreement coming unglued, despite the facts that termination of a line is always going to be a possibility. At the same time, the rep who negotiates a sales agreement without a reasonable severance provision in the contract is a man who must think there is no tomorrow. You don't have to be a cynic about it but you should use hard-nosed business sense in assuming that the cheery, hip-hip-hooray camaraderie in which you and your new sales manager have just come to accord, could very well some day wind up in a melancholy togethermess.

It may be difficult to get the kind of termination understanding you would like but manufacturers are more and more realizing their obligations and the rightfulness of compensating those who have contributed to the growth of their business. It should not be impossible to incorporate details for terminating a rep arrangement in a fair and equitable manner. But, of course, there is no one standardized way to do it.

Many formulas have been devised; in each case it becomes necessary to negotiate the termination provision, usually starting with the time of representation as a basis. No one has a definitive for you but, by way of example, the formula contrived by the Electronic Representatives Association to which I referred in "The Manufacturers' Representative" is still, to my way of thinking, entirely reasonable for both principal and representative. Basically, it provides that the terminated rep receive one month's severance pay for each of two full years during which he served as the manufacturer's representative. It establishes a maximum number of months (i.e., 12 months) for such to be paid and that each payment be 1/12 of the total commissions paid the rep in the twelve months preceding his termination.

It is difficult to see why any fair minded, right thinking manufacturer should object to incorporating such a formula into the agreement with the rep at the time the sales contract is first set up.

Occasionally a rep sure of his capabilities and eager to get a certain line he's learned is open, will issue a challenge to the prospective principal — that his firm be allowed to handle the line for a stated period, perhaps six months, maybe a year. He predicts he will produce some specified substantial amount of business within that time and, upon making good, is then to be considered the regular rep for that territory from then on.

To undertake a kind of trial marriage like this is impressive with its show of self-confidence. Besides, it is reassuring to the sales manager who, in making a new appointment, regardless of how promising the firm may appear to be, is taking a certain amount of gamble that he is getting the kind of representation he wants. *However,* a rep entering into such a tentative sales arrangement, should assume it *will* work out as he expected and, *right in the beginning* ought to negotiate the regular representation contract, complete in all details, including a fair termination understanding, its finalization being dependent only upon his having performed for the temporary period as agreed. Otherwise, once he's started to be identified with the line, he is no longer in a good position to insist on some provision he believes should be included — he's just about going to have to take what he's given. Besides, the inconclusive state of their agreement leaves open the possibility of other reps coming into the picture. What the deal should come to is that the contract be drawn up in full on a (so-called) permanent basis *with the understanding* that if the rep has not produced as agreed within the stated period the arrangement may be automatically dissolved without recriminations.

An arrangement for continuance or renewal of a contract based on the rep producing a certain minimum sales volume within a stated period of time, (the amount depending on the status of the line at the time of negotiations) would seem to be very fair to all concerned. If the volume specified appears practical and reasonable, presumably a rep should not object. But it has at least one bad aspect. If, for any reason of his own, a manufacturer wants to rid himself of a rep, this clause makes it readily feasible for him to do so. He can delay shipments, instigate errors in invoicing and other paper work, neglect the rep's correspondence and by other devious means handicap the rep to a quitting point while short of the specified volume of sales.

A rep friend of mine with that kind of arrangement in one case, told me quite recently of a distressing incident leading to being incredibly terminated, with such a "minimum volume per year" clause providing the excuse. After intensive negotiation with a major customer for almost a year, he had finally taken a huge order, to start with a small initial shipment, the balance to follow after the sample amount was received and approved. Just about that time his principal replaced the elderly, veteran sales manager with a newcomer, a younger man on whom the president was very much sold up, telling the reps that the new man was expected to pep up the organization with his youthful drive, would introduce all

kinds of new plans and, altogether, was going to make lots
and lots of money for everybody around there.

The initial amount against the big order wasn't being
shipped. Both the customer and the rep expedited but got
only an inexplicable run-around. When the rep phoned, the
sales manager was "out" — and his calls weren't being returned. Worse yet, neither were the customer's wires and
phone calls answered. Finally, the buyer got his back up, told
the rep he was being offered an equivalent product by a
competitor and gave my rep friend a deadline to either
deliver or he'd cancel the order and buy from the competitor.

Desperate, with thousands of dollars in commissions hanging in the balance, the rep hopped a plane back to the
factory. As he entered the offices, through a door into the
warehouse swinging open, he could see shelves filled with the
very items on which his customer was waiting.

"Yup," the sales manager replied smugly to his query.
"We've got 'em in stock." But the quotation made before (by
his predecessor) was, in *his* opinion, ridiculously low, that the
customer *had* to use this particular item and could be
"worked" to pay more, that the competitor's product wasn't
as good, that if they just stalled delivery for a while longer
until the customer had no other choice, he would be amena-
ble to paying a higher price on the item.

The rep couldn't believe his own ears. The president of the
company was away, touring somewhere in Europe. There was
no one to whom he could appeal. The sales manager was
adamant — he'd show some of the old fossils around here
how to really make money.

It was hopeless. The outcome? The customer cancelled and
bought from the competitor, as he had threatened, it being
simple — the competitor had only to follow what the rep, the
customer's and the factory's engineers had worked up during
the preceding year. The business fell into the competitor's lap
like ripe fruit . . . . The aftermath? The rep didn't make the
contract quota amount that year; the discussions, the recrimi-

nations and the chagrin at losing the big order resulted in the sales manager making him the fall guy, and he was fired.

It takes two to tangle; hold your temper!

If a man isn't dying from an incurable disease and if he has not yet lived to an over-ripe age, one may presume he still has a future somewhere in the offing and ought to govern himself accordingly. But—one sometimes wonders about how many people there are around so singularly myopic when it comes to looking beyond their noses. Lack of foresight seems to show up so often in many who find themselves in an adverse situation, who fail to accept the fact that the current wretchedness, whatever it may be, is a passing experience and, hopefully, one may expect better things sooner or later. The need for keeping your cool is an observance particularly relevant in this often trying rep occupation; it applies especially to that built-in hazard of manufacturers' representation, the tragically common experience of being terminated on a desirable line. A f'r instance:

A rep of my acquaintance had been working a certain line profitably for a number of years, presumably to the satisfaction of all concerned. Came a year when the factory's overall business nationally fell off. The company's stockholders began clamoring; the officer brass was concerned but, as came out later, unaware during that year of the real reason for the drop in sales volume.

The next year, business fell still further although, as it happened, volume was holding up quite well in this rep's territory, largely because of several sizeable accounts established long years before. In consequence, to his amazement, one day the rep received a "Dear John" letter, giving him thirty days notice that his services were no longer required. The explanation: new policy — as a presumed economy measure, the company was replacing all of its representatives with "direct" factory salesmen.

Now, as is always so highly publicized when it happens,

the change of a manufacturer from commissioned sales representatives to "direct" factory employed salesmen, is no novelty in this business. It will happen when the manufacturer chooses to disregard the work done by the reps in building up the territories and stems from the fact that the principal thinks the rep is making too much money in return for devoting only a portion of the day's working time to the line. He reasons he can hire a man to work on his line all day exclusively and for no more money than he has been paying the rep.

But — what does *not* get equal airing for some reason or other is the fact that the manufacturer making the change to "direct" in almost every case eventually learns he has made a bad mistake as sales volume falls off drastically in the territory formerly represented by the independent professional salesman. Before long, he is confronted with more difficulties than a hula dancer suffering from arthritis. In due time, "face" permitting, he is very likely to go back to the former commission rep system, a good possibility of which most experienced reps are aware.

Is it politic, then, to go on the warpath upon being terminated, knocking the factory, its personnel, perhaps even the products? Suppose the customers now become aware of how the terminated rep feels about his erstwhile principal. Is it wise to create the possibility of the trade wondering how come he represented so lousy an outfit in the first place?

And, another suppose: how about the sales manager being criticized outspokenly for the termination? May he not have friends among *other* sales managers and, as can happen, the terminated rep's name comes up. Can't you just visualize the kind of a chopping up that rep could get?

As to the case I have been relating: the incensed rep blew his top, apparently justified because the termination was so irrational under the circumstances. Not being particularly bright, it didn't occur to this fellow that since there was nothing to lose, he might have gone over the sales manager's head to the company's president (whom he had met several times) with the possibility of persuading the chief executive to question the firing of a rep who had been doing so well for the company. He did indeed pick up the phone and called the president but, instead of playing it cool, gave wrathful vent to his feelings. Before the other could say a word, he plunged into a profane tirade, telling the officer what he thought of his company, of the crummy sales manager, of their lousy products, and particularly of this company head who didn't have sense enough to appreciate a good man — etc., etc., until the president hung up on him. He turned from the phone, filled with self-righteous satisfaction, the ends of justice presumably having been served by what he had told that so and so.

Of course that was the end of his affiliation with *that* line. But: what the rep hadn't realized nor allowed for was that the company's president had been working night and day, devoting every waking minute to searching out the reasons for the national fall-off of business. He learned! It was finally revealed that the sales manager was an alcoholic, that he was paying less and less attention to his duties. Underlings had been carrying on the company's affairs without the experience or direction required; in this instance, an assistant had made the change to "direct" factory employed salesmen which the sales manager, in a drunken stupor, had approved. Soon thereafter, the sales manager fired, sure enough the manufacturer went back to the commissioned rep system.

Did the hot-headed erstwhile rep get the line back? You mean — after that phone call to that president? What do you think?

Another kind of insurance?

Some reps anticipate a possible termination notice by indirect means. I remember hearing of one cynic, active in consumer products, who made a practice of accumulating as many samples of his principals' products as possible, wherever the items had substantial intrinsic value. His reasoning was that in the event of being unfairly terminated, he would have enough of the principal's goods on hand ("possession is nine points of the law") to help enforce his attempts to make the principal deal fairly with him!

Another philosophy is that of the rep who believes the possibility of being "terminated" unfairly adds to the need for closely studying the lines of manufacturers competitive to your principal — for reasons aside from the benefits of knowing the competition as an aid to your selling. That is, should a contract be cancelled on you, and you feel you were not treated right, he reasons that what you already know about equivalent lines can prove of inestimable value when you consider trying to pick up a line to replace the one lost. After all, he points out, you are in a key position — knowing the trade, the better customers, where the bodies are buried, making of you a desirable addition to one of your former principal's competitors.

What can you do when the sky falls?
A certain very promising manufacturer had excellent products and good ideas for more to come, but in his early years was woefully inexperienced when it came to marketing. Aside from functioning for him in the usual rep capacity, one of his reps, a widely experienced and personal friend of long standing, was frequently consulted for advice on the mechanics of expanding his business from a thriving local affair to a full-fledged national operation. As time went by, on a number of occasions he called upon the same rep's aid in solving marketing problems that had him stymied. The rep had a hand in the development of his catalog into a comprehensive publication, that being one of this rep's specialties. He persuaded the manufacturer to change his marketing approach from one class of trade to another, a move soon to reflect

itself in increased sales volume. Although his monetary remuneration was only the regular rep commission, during the nine years this man repped the line and happily watched it grow, just the feeling that he had a substantial part in this progress was great for his ego. Nor was his friend, the manufacturer, at all averse to voicing gratitude, telling people that this rep's ideas, criticisms and suggestions had helped him beyond measure.

So what happened to this rep and this line? I'll bet, if you are an old timer, you're way ahead of me! You know why I'm telling this story! and, you're right! Came that bleak day when the said rep received the stiffly formal notification, signed by a name new to him, that his representation of this factory was to terminate as of thirty days from date, and would he please prepare the samples for picking up by the representative appointed to replace him. True story! Period!

What do you do in a case like that — or whenever you part company with a manufacturer involuntarily, so to speak? Do you rave and rant or break down and cry? Make cynical cracks about friendships? Laugh and play the good loser bit? Or do you become more determined than ever to make damned sure that any future sales contracts into which you enter will have to provide a reasonably compensatory period in the event of termination, including a scale of residual payment proportioned to the time in which you were a rep?

There is such a thing as representation relationships going on and on, seemingly never to end. On the other hand, you may variously find it necessary to resign a line because the manufacturer just couldn't keep up with competition, for lack of factory cooperation, because new product developments were making one principal's devices competitive with one of your other lines, because of unreasonably dragging out the time of commission payments . . . or whatever.

But it is the arbitrary *dismissals* that try the rep's soul. When one of your important lines is undergoing a change of sales managers, it could mean you will be going through a change of life somewhat on the early side. Your friendly buddy-buddy sales manager is fired or resigns and his successor brings in a favorite of his own to supplant you. A short sighted sales manager resents the size of the commissions you are earning and switches your territory to a direct factory employed salesman. Business suffers because of managerial mistakes but, to save face, the blame is placed on you and you become a fatality. Not at all uncommon are those heart breakers resulting from mergers, as was the case in the incident I just described, wherein the subject manufacturers' company was merged with another, much larger, and a new sales management group was formed, to move in and take over. Two sets of reps were one too many and so the first group got kicked out. The manufacturer couldn't help it — he no longer had control.

Manufacturers' representation is no place for a pessimist but you do have to be a *realist*. It takes the maturity that develops from experience to meet the exigencies of life with practical philosophy. The professional in manufacturers' representation utilizes all his know-how and extends every effort entailed in doing a good job assuming, with reasonable justification, that if he produces the results, it becomes awfully hard, if not impossible, to replace him. While from every standpoint, his own and in the interests of his principals, the pro gives the work all he's got, but at the same time he never stops being on the lookout for the possibility of adding desirable lines to his roster. He is not impelled by greed or disloyalty to his current principals but as a pragmatist, he realizes self-preservation makes it necessary to protect himself from the disastrous possibilities of losing an important line by being sufficiently cushioned with enough lines to absorb the shock.

Not to digress, but that brings up a related point on which reps may honestly disagree — referring to those who get up extremely attractive presentations describing their activities, intended to impress prospective principals. These may be printed folders or even quite elaborate, expensive brochures. But the question arises about this fancy example of the printer's craft: what effect does it have on one's current principals? Or future ones, for that matter. Is it wise to let manufacturers know you are *always* hunting more lines, that this is a fixed practice, that you regularly spend substantial amounts of money in the search? A principal may ask himself, what's wrong with your present roster of lines — especially, *his* — heh? Does this policy signify that you play put and take with lines, he asks?

Instead of a generalized formal presentation of the firm's operations, the other approach is this: keep on tap a compilation of all those salient points and favorable features about your firm in which you feel a manufacturer seeking representation would be interested. Then, when you've made contact with a prospective principal, put these "salient points" etc. into a personally typed letter, one written especially to and for him.

The difference? A printed form soliciting lines may raise skepticism in your principal's minds, which won't do you any good — whereas a letter describing your qualifications would be entirely normal, to be expected and judged on *its wording* rather than the distracting brochure or folder picturing your operation. ☐

IV

BIGGER AND BETTER – HOW?

Beyond the horizon – off-shore opportunities

It took some years to do it but now you've got a pretty good roster of lines. You have one or two salesmen, hard workers, between you producing a fine volume of business. Your secretary is a jewel and, with the part-time girl helping her, holds down the office routine in good shape. In short; you've got an excellent business going and would be very pleased with yourself except for one thing: you're not rich – yet. And, you'd like to be. But at the rate you're going – ?

A rep who has built up a business to a point where it can be described as per above, must be already doing more things right than wrong. Particularly, he will have become aware that the road to riches is paved with good lines. He's learned of how to go about acquiring lines by advertising, by attending conventions, by publicizing, by studying trade publications, by referrals from people favorably inclined to him, by the reputation he's established – and all the rest of it. He knows all too well that desirable lines are hard to come by. What *else* – can he do in the way of acquiring good lines?

There is another, a *good* possibility. He can raise his horizons – look beyond American shores – to Europe, to Latin America, to Asia, to Canada . . . And – if you'll forgive the pun – representing foreign countries isn't as outlandish as you might think. It has some *very* interesting aspects.

America has been facing up to the fact that its much vaunted mass production methods and technical know-how are no longer exclusive advantages, that foreign countries are now well able to compete with us right on our own home grounds. Japan, Germany and England aren't the only nations who have successfully entered our commercial distribution channels. Those pretty little brass ashtrays from India, candy from Switzerland, cash registers from Sweden, shoes from Italy — but why go on — we're all familiar now with the fact that huge inroads have been made into American business by foreign manufacturers. Not only that but, ironically enough, it was this country that helped immeasurably to create that competition. All of which brings about the pragmatic philosophy: if you can't lick 'em, join 'em. Why not?

When I was a young man, Japan was like light years away; today we measure the distance in hours. Germany was a far off place you studied about in school or, later, you might go there to fight a war. Today, no longer are other countries removed from our everyday intercourse; America has come out of isolation from the rest of the world. Europe, Asia, South America — the aeroplane and modern communication have made us all neighbors. Our commercial lives intertwine. It is no more a novelty to find your acquaintances are doing business with foreign countries; you know that when a man says he's just returned from a business trip to Paris, he probably doesn't mean the Paris in Texas or the one in Tennessee or Illinois or Kentucky or Arkansas, but that he is referring to *the* Paris and everyone knows where *that* is!

To get into the business of representing one or more foreign country manufacturers won't be too easy, but how about the lines you now have? Was it easy getting them? And, when you chose to become a rep, you knew one has to dig to get the gold out of a mine, didn't you? So — if you're ready to try, there are some fine tools available.

You can go one or more of several ways. One is to contact **the foreign consular offices** in the United States to ask their assistance in making contact with manufacturers in *their* countries who might be interested in arranging for American representation. The key man in these offices is the *commercial attache* (or he may be known by some synonymous term). These men are appointed by their governments for the special purposes of fostering their countries' trade so, in most cases, your interest should be welcome. You can get a list of these offices from the **"Superintendent of Documents,"** Government **Printing Office, Washington, D.C. 20420** at forty-five cents a copy.

Speaking of gold, the U.S. Department of Commerce's **Bureau of International Commerce, Washington, D.C. 20230,** is able and willing to be a mine of information. All it takes is your enquiry to start getting to the precious metal. It is that BIC's job to foster international trade and they have all kinds of very practical and applicable material available. Just as one example: I saw recently a copy of their "INTERNATIONAL COMMERCE" reprint entitled, "125 Trade Offices in the U.S. listed for 60 nations." Such "trade" offices can supply you with a wealth of information about their countries of special interest to Americans seeking to establish commercial relations with them.

By way of further help: contact the **Department of Commerce Field Office** in your city, if one is there. (BIC can give you a list of these office addresses.) Or, get in touch directly with the **"Commercial Intelligence Division," Bureau of International Commerce, U.S. Dept. of Commerce, Washington, D.C. 20230.** Just tell them in so many words what you are after. That department has available trade lists which are highly informative. For example, they can give you foreign firms listed by name, mailing address, name and title of chief executive, function, type of organization, date of establishment, size, numbers of employees. When requesting such "trade lists," specify the industry in which you are interested, i.e., scientific instruments, houseware, electronics, hardware and so on. A charge of $1.00 per country for each principal industry category is made.

Suppose you want information about a specific firm. "World Trade Directory Reports" are available from BIC at $2.00 each. These are not credit reports, although they do give the names and addresses of credit information sources. But a typical report describes the type of organization, method of operation, size of firm, kind of products, names of officers, capital, sales volume, general reputation in trade and financial circles — just the kind of information you normally look for when taking on a domestic line.

Special "Trade Contact Surveys" in the way of marketing data and searching out firms who might meet your specific requirements is another BIC service. It's almost like having your own man over there, except that BIC knows immediately where to go to dig up the information requested. A charge of $50 is made per survey.

A great variety of valuable literature is available from the U.S. Department of Commerce. There are publications giving trade statistics, economic data about the country in which you are interested. You can get BIC's "Worldwide Exhibitions Schedule," comprising over 800 general and specialized trade fairs quite similar to our own conventions or trade shows so common in this country. At today's reasonable flight rates (plus being a write-off) you would do well to take this route, to see with your own eyes what is offered, and very likely pick up one or more lines right there on the spot.

Still another assist angle: if you would want to make a trip overseas as a scouting preliminary for the purpose of negotiating trade connections, BIC will help you meet the kind of businessmen whom you would want to contact. But to arrange this, get in touch with your nearest Department of

Commerce Field Office at least a month before you want to take off.

As to how the moneys involved would be handled: the BIC can give you fully detailed information about methods of payment, letters of credit, foreign exchange risks, sight and time drafts, special banking arrangements, how to handle goods (whether through specializing brokers or yourself), government regulations and other pertinent data.

Also, just to start looking abroad: a couple of the airline companies, by way of promoting their own business, maintain periodically revised lists of foreign country business people seeking to make contact with American businessmen. Pan-American is one in particular who makes quite an elaborate presentation of helping bring about such rapprochement. A call to one of their offices should get you their willing help. After all, they'd like to make you a passenger — the obvious name of their game.

It doesn't take too much imagination to envision the outgrowth of several possibilities. You may, for example, start just on the basis of repping a given line on the usual commission basis — you get the orders, the manufacturer ships and collects. Later, it may prove worth while for you to stock the line in this country, opening possibilities for overrides, for receiving warehouse fees, for filling the orders yourself at a distributor's profit rather than only the rep commission.

Another possible twist: because of import duty considerations or for any one of several reasons, looking abroad might lead to *you* importing components parts for, in turn, assembling them yourself here into the complete device. There are some outstanding examples of rep firms already going this extremely interesting route.

Other potentially beneficial arrangements could develop.

As you feel more at home dealing with foreign principals and with the requirements of foreign countries, you may even consider going in for *exporting*—an entirely different kind of mining operation but one from which you might dig up some very high assay ore.

For instance — as just one of many possibilities — one of your domestic principals may have a series of products that lends itself to promoting in other countries. He hasn't done anything about that aspect of his business. Well — how about you getting into it? As you come to know foreign business-men at close hand during your repping operations, opportunities could very well appear for working together in other ways. This is not at all too far fetched, if you will just give it a little thought. Consider a few facts at random:

> The U.S.A. is still the world's largest exporter, to the tune of almost 50 billions dollars a year, growing at the rate of 11% each year but — get this! only 4% of American firms do all that business — *plus the fact that more than three out of five exporters employ less than 100 people!* How do the competitive odds compare in your present activity?

> Now — just for fun — let's suppose you know of a product or series of items which you think might sell in foreign countries but, we'll presume you know little or nothing about the mechanics of selling abroad. Okay — you contact the U.S. Department of Commerce, who will put you in touch with various export managing firms specializing in getting newcomers started through the presumed intricacies of dealing with foreign countries. You would soon learn the few applicable routines required and then take over yourself, eliminating their fees.

> Or, another approach: if you want to check into

possibilities for exporting, you can join a "Trade Mission" under the auspices of the Department of Commerce and travel overseas with the "Mission" to make commercial contacts. (And, of course, travelling for business is a deductible). If of interest, contact the Department for details. Likewise — if you prefer hopping a plane alone to take a good hard look for yourself, right on the premises, the Department has 468 commercial and economic offices attached to 152 U.S. Embassies and Consulates to arrange help for you when you are there.

Major banks are ready, willing and anxious to help finance interesting projects, to handle funds in international trade and in many ways maintain services to guide exporters.

If, as and when you have products ready to sell abroad, you can rent space for as little as $400 at a Commerce Department Trade Center in Europe, Asia, Australia and Latin America, through the Bureau of International Commerce, c/o U.S. Department of Commerce.

Note, too, that some unique tax advantages are available for exporters such as, at this writing, taxes can be deferred on 50% of export profits.

Well, I am quite sure that, with some exceptions, the idea of a rep going in for importing or exporting, is foreign, indeed (joke!). So was selling refrigerators to Eskimos once a joke. My point is that one thing leads to another and getting started on one angle of foreign business can bring up other possibilities.

SO — why not raise your sights and take a few squints beyond the horizon? After all, with seven-eighths of the total world market lying outside of the United States, do you *have* to limit your efforts to only one-eighth of all that available territory?   □

V

INVENTORYING

A rewarding practice

Needless to say, if you sell through distributors, your fate with a line is dependent on how extensively they stock it in quantity and diversity. Nothing so irritates a would-be customer like trying to order an item from a so-called "franchised" distributor, supposedly carrying a full stock, only to find "it's out of stock." The excuses he gets are seldom in your favor. He is told, "the factory is slow in delivery," "the item isn't popular so we don't stock it" or they substitute a competitive brand for the call-out.

Yourself inventorying your distributors periodically and seeing to it that they maintain proper stock levels is, of course, one and usually a successful way to meet the problem. Aside from the actual counting, a big assist however is for you to keep current inventory records of each distributor's stock *in your office*. With every piece of promotional material, in whatever mailers you send to the trade, as well as in person, encourage the trade to *call your office* if they are having difficulty locating one of your products. Tell it to them! Emphasize your desire to help, informing them that you have such records at your fingertips, that you can advise them immediately who has the desired item in stock.

Not only does the customer appreciate your assistance but the results can provide you with some excellent selling ammunition as, for instance, in the case of a distributor whom you have been trying to persuade to stock a given item. You might be able to tell him that, in actual fact, you are getting calls, in some cases, from *his* customers seeking the referenced item and that you (so regretfully!) have had to refer the callers to one of this distributor's competitors, who *does* normally carry the item in stock, enjoys a good sale on it, etc., etc. Along the same lines, a new development may have calls starting for an item which none of the distributors have been stocking, thus alerting you to its sudden demand and providing the information to, in turn, pass on to your distributors. A big point in keeping such records is the plus it becomes with your principal, he being pleased to see you giving his line such special attention.

In any event, it is a graphic instance of rendering the very real service to the trade that, so often, is only talked about.

☐

VI

DEAR MR. SALES MANAGER

WHAT IT REALLY TAKES TO ATTRACT THE BETTER REPS

The able sales manager capable of arousing interest in his line among the better rep firms when requiring the services of a sales representative, would himself know what it means to be a manufacturers' representative — which is not at all the simplistic statement it seems to be. If he's good at his job, he will attract the better reps because he is one who realizes what really motivates and goes on in the minds of sales representatives. He'd be one who would display comprehension which encourages, stimulates — his empathy to bring on a degree of appreciation and loyalty from reps bound to help them both advance to their mutual goals. Unfortunately, such knowledgeable, understanding men don't come along too often.

I have often wondered what criteria (if any!) were used for making the sales manager appointments in the instances of some manufacturers with whom I have come in contact. There was that character, newly appointed by a New York manufacturer, whom I met for the first time upon his arrival in San Francisco. We sat at the bar in his hotel where, his tongue loosened up after a number of drinks, he told me that instead of calling on them in person, he'd take care of the customers by phone, that he wanted to use his time to see the sights. He scarcely tried to conceal the fact that he had taken the job only to get a paid-for trip to California! that upon his return to New York, he was taking over a restaurant deal there awaiting him!

Admittedly an extreme case — usually the misfits to whom I refer weren't necessarily unscrupulous or stupid — there were among them those who had impressive track records in the way of business experience. Their problem was inability to grasp the nature *of the rep.*

The man who chooses to become a manufacturers' representative is not an ordinary man!

It is a bad break — for both *his reps and his company — when, as can happen, some twist of Fate places an unqualified man in the position of sales manager, one who may start with a big bang, only to fizzle out like so much soda water gone flat and sour. But, as any experienced rep can testify, it is all too frequently the lack of know-how in dealing with independent professional salesmen that causes many sales managers to fall down on their jobs. I say this without rancor. Of the sales managers a rep gets to know, there may be and often are (as this writer can personally testify) some of the finest men one can hope to meet, but just because they are "nice guys" doesn't make them* effective *managers.*

It could *be the newcomer, inexperienced in sales managership, who has problems attracting the independent professional salesmen but, regretfully, examples can be found among men who have been in that position for many years — especially those whose methods in appointing reps are based on trial and error instead of from in-depth understanding of the manufacturers' representative. As in any attempt to deal successfully with people, some knowledge of human nature is mandatory — in this case, especially to be aware of the highly individualistic spirit which makes the rep an anomaly among sales people.*

What KIND of man goes in for repping? Know this:

The man who eschews being an employee, who chooses manufacturers' representation as an occupation, is bound to be a decisive person. He knows what he likes and what he wants. He's not the kind to be happy leading a sedentary life. He doesn't relish sitting at a desk even though entirely cognizant of the fact that a critical import of his work is to carry on as a regional sales manager. He chafes at office routine, bewails the piling up of paper work, longs to be out in the field where he can be "up and at 'em" but, at the same time, pitches into functioning as the executive administrative head of his enterprise.

In his latter capacity, the absolute life or death of his chosen occupation is embodied in the process of selecting the manufacturers whom he will represent. And he *does* pick and choose! The frequently heard, wailing cliche, "lines are hard to get," can be very deceiving to sales managers complacently conscious of their power in the dispensation of lines. They should realize that the rep's plaint is not necessarily from hunger, but is preceded by the inferred "GOOD" lines being the scarce ones. In most industries, it is unlikely that more than a tenth (if that many) of the thousands of lines available are considered "good." There are limits to how many lines can be handled to advantage by the number of reps operating in a given territory.

Clearly, the better rep is going to be choosy.

Consider, too, the rep type doesn't do things the easiest way because that's the way "they" do it, it being the nature of the rep to be innovative, to pioneer, to travel his own chosen routes. He has disdained the anonymity of the corporation job, of being relegated to a depersonalized set of digits programmed into an inhuman company computer. He resents being classed as a statistic, insisting upon being known as an entity in himself.

Does all this mean he has plenty of ego? Asserts himself; even though soft-spoken, usually manages to make himself heard in a crowd? Wants to know *why* he is asked to do something, as well as what, before he decides whether or not he will do it? Yes — right! You'd better believe it! Though he exudes self-confidence — and with due allowance for the exceptions bound to show up when voicing a generality — he is not at all necessarily offensive, but false modesty is not likely to be a characteristic of the man who has chosen to be "self-employed" . . . .

It is the independent professional salesman's very personal characteristics that are so advantageous to his principals. Though often a visionary, he combined head-in-the-clouds dreams with the earthiness of door-to-door selling, working with all he's got to promote ethereal ideas into solid accomplishment. That he is operating a well established, good going business (unless he merely inherited it or bought it from somebody else) means you can well accept and take for granted that he must be self-motivated, foresighted in realistic long-range planning, and possessed of a good understanding of marketing's complexities because *those are basic requirements in building a rep business.*

THE INDEPENDENT MANUFACTURERS' SALES REPRESENTATIVE IS AMONG THE LAST OF THOSE IMBUED WITH THE PIONEERING SPIRIT, THE ENTREPRENEUR WHO BROUGHT THIS COUNTRY TO GREATNESS, WITH EACH GENERATION BECOMING MORE AND MORE UNCOMMON—NAMELY, THE INDEPENDENT SMALL BUSINESSMAN.

*   *   *

Who are you? the rep wants to know

Enthroned on his Olympian heights, the sales manager knows he is in a position of might, being able to place a line with whom he pleases or take it away at his will, and that the rep who gets the line is, because of this largesse, so very lucky to be going to make money for himself out of it. In some cases, this can be pretty heady stuff, liable to unbalance a sales manager with inferences of having ten-foot stature in the scheme of things. Then, too, in carrying out the critical functions of securing the most desirable reps, although he has every good intention, a sales manager may just not be aware of all the facets a rep has to look at before he can even *start* to consider a new line. As a very common instance of misunderstanding: when a territory is open and the sales manager has secured the names of a number of reps (by means to be touched on later), he writes them letters of which the following is typical, word for word:

> *Dear Mr. Repper:*
>
> *We are seeking a representative in your territory to sell our watchamatronics. If you are interested, please let us have a list of your lines, a description of the territory you cover and names of the accounts you call on, details of your personnel, how long in business and any other information you can supply which will help us judge your suitability.*
>
> *Yours very truly,*
> *THE WHOZIS COMPANY*
> *By Mr. Talk Little,*
> *Sales Manager*

You can believe me when I say every established rep has seen innumerable letters like that, maddening in their superficiality, supplying nothing beyond a barely mentioned reference to what gidgets the manufacturer makes and specifying

no more than his name about who he is — while yet asking
the rep to supply information not much short of the story of
his life. And the pity of it is, despite the "Thanks — but no,
thanks" responses he receives, or even no answers at all from
reps who can't take the time to go hunting for possible
buried treasure on the basis of such meager information, the
sales manager doesn't know why he isn't getting shows of
interest in his line. It just doesn't seem to occur to him that
he is emulating an employer who posts a "help wanted" sign,
then sits back waiting for the line of applicants to form.
Since there are always reps around who will take on anything
that comes along, eventually he gets somebody but all too
often he has to settle for a less capable rep than he would like
to have had, simply because he did not use the approach that
would draw the attention of the better reps.

Let's say you're the sales manager of a company employing several hundred people and doing a nice, multi-million
dollars a year. Certainly, yours is no two-bit operation and
you assume your line should be highly interesting to reps.
Very likely, it could be — but, unless your company is
actually "big" enough for its name to be a byword in your
industry, the chances are that, across the country, many reps
never heard of it! Even within the limits of one industry,
there can be thousands of manufacturers, some quite sizeable, of whom only a minor number would be widely known.

Or — suppose your company's name *is* somewhat familiar.
You just have to understand that merely the name of your
company, a word or two about what you produce and the
fact that you need representation, don't add up to enough
for creating clap hands excitement in the life of the *established* rep. It takes more than that — such as starting with
some display of empathy on your part.

If you are soliciting a busy rep's time for the purpose of
taking up the possibilities of him representing you, he will
need some initial assurance that you know how to work with

reps, as would be shown by supplying enough preliminary information to indicate you do understand sales manufacturers' representation. What is important to remember is that the manufacturers' representative is unique in that, once a sales agreement is made, aside from his own business, he becomes identified with his principal's management and, to some extent, the factory's engineering. In short, he becomes a member of the family. That being the case:

When you come to terms with a long established, experienced rep, it follows that you are acquiring the services of a sales expert, a consultant, a knowledgeable man in the territory, of one who has put in years learning the ins and outs of selling, who understands the quirks of the trade, who knows where to put in extensive sales effort and where to refrain from wasting time, who stands ready to foster and protect your interests at all times, who becomes a local authority for you in the territory to whom the trade can turn for help on your products, who seeks out the hidden corners and the byways where he introduces your wares to trade who perhaps had never heard of you and, Mister, pay attention! — are you ready? — YOU GET ALL THIS EXPERTISE HELP AND WORK *FOR FREE!* Yup, for nothing — his services don't cost your company one thin dime! The only time you have to put out any money to this man is only after he has placed orders for your goods on your desk!

Consider this: say your tax consultant, your lawyer — do any professionals give you the benefit of their time, know-how and work at no charge, as does the manufacturers' sales representative? Is it reasonable to expect that a man so qualified, potentially ready to do so much for his principals, will get all choked up because somebody or other he perhaps never heard of happens to send him a note saying a representative is wanted?

*   *   *

Another point to keep in mind for the sales manager seeking the best representation: in the event of it becoming known that his line is "up for grabs" and because there *are* many reps who may stretch grasping hands for it, doesn't mean it will be easy for him to get the kind of rep he really wants — not, that is, just because there are so many available.

Let's assume it becomes known that an interesting line is "open" and that a goodly number of reps will be contacting the sales manager, who then has this lot of applicants from whom to make his selection. Unfortunately, manufacturers' representation has its share of misfits, attracted by what superficially appears to be an easy life occupation. Among them, assuredly will be those who, no matter how incompetent otherwise, know the value of flattery, that "it will get you everywhere." It is one of the oldest and most effective weapons in the salesman's arsenal because, even when recognized as such, to be the object of flattery is like getting splashed with paint — you can brush most of it off but some of it is bound to stick. Very often, it is the favorite, ingratiating ploy used by those indiscriminant reps who jump at the chance to acquire a new line without taking the time to evaluate it properly.

Now, the mere fact that a rep makes himself agreeable and shows, frankly, he is interested in the line, certainly is not in itself a reason for ruling him in or out. But the thoughtful sales manager will be smart to consider especially the conservative rep, the one who does *not* commit himself right off the reel, the one whose deliberating attitude indicates it is just as much *his* decision whether or not *he* will join in with you, as it is your privilege to question appointing him. And don't be annoyed if his approach includes searching and, very often, what may appear to be highly personal questions.

Suppose your sales were off last year — lower than the year before. Why? Are you losing ground to competition? Internal problems? Are you well capitalized? Willing to supply a financial statement? How long has your factory been in existence? How long have *you* had the job of sales manager?

And so on. Such extended inquiries are characteristic of the thorough, deep delving *professional* salesman.

To sum up to that point: the better rep whose interest you have attracted by the kind of detailed letter to be described later, will make every effort to learn what kind of principal this is likely to be, to ascertain whether the line is worthy of being added to those he already carries, whether or not the potential is there to warrant the time and promotion he puts into his lines. You can almost bank on it that the rep who grabs your line without taking the time to explore it will be the one you will soon fire or he will quit you before very long, and you'll have it all to go through all over again. The rep who, along with your main requirements, indicates by his deliberation that he is experienced, has a sense of responsibility, is cautious about committing himself, thinks in terms of long range, is the one you'd do well to appoint — if he is willing — because that is the kind of rep who produces the results most likely to make your principal-representative relationship successful.

In approaching prospective reps

Before getting into the positive details desirable in contacting reps, let's take a moment for the negative inducing kind of communication from a sales manager seeking representation, an approach which really sets the rep's teeth on edge. This is the one which starts with a formal resume-questionnaire for the rep to fill out. In the first place, the very fact of being asked to apply for the line by way of a written form immediately brings up the *inference* of an employer-employee relationship. To the rep who went into business for himself, largely motivated by the desire to be his own boss, such resumes are too reminiscent of the world he left behind. This is the sort of thing *he* may require of a prospective secretary or other office help perhaps. But for himself, he feels he is beyond such things; he may fill it out but he won't like it.

An ire arousing question characteristic of such resumes, though also sometimes asked verbally, is the one pertaining to his sales volume. He is likely to volunteer a total over all figure as proof of what big business he does for his principals. However, what does burn him up — but let me give you the essence of an actual incident from my own experience, typical of this request to divulge proprietory information:

This was the sales manager of a nationally very well known company, in town seeking representation, and we were seated in his hotel room for the interview. We had just covered a few generalities about each other when the phone rang. The call was from another rep scheduled to be interviewed and that man was now in the lobby waiting to come up.

"I've got to see him," he said, "but I've heard about you and I'm interested in your firm." He sorted through his brief case and came up with a two-page form which he handed to me. "Take this along with you and bring it by tomorrow filled out, when we can carry on at leisure."

My eyes ran over it. Two questions hit me right away — the first about halfway down the first page. It read, "State your gross annual sales for the past three years." That was reasonable but then, after a number of otherwise more-or-less standard questions, on the second page, with obvious intent deliberately separated far from the first about sales volume so that, presumably, the applicant wouldn't connect the two, came the question, "Name your three main lines in order of sales volume and give the percentage each one bears to your total gross sales."

That was all I needed to tell me this line was not for me. I did not think the second question proper and I particularly resented the tricky way in which it was positioned. I held his form out to him. He looked at me questioningly "I'd rather not state how much business is being done by each of three principals in this territory," I said, "whose products are in no way competitive with yours. If I were representing you, would you want me to reveal freely to anybody just how much business you were doing in this territory?" I added that I'd be glad to give him my *total* gross sales but that I felt my duty to my current principals made it necessary to treat their individual sales figures as confidential.

"I've given you a list of my principals," I said. "You are welcome to contact any or all of them, to ask what kind of job we do for them. Any information *they* want to give you *themselves* along the lines you are asking for, is for *them* to decide. There are ways for you to evaluate a prospective rep," I continued, "without prying into matters which could hardly be expected to affect your business." I handed him back his form, uttered a few more conventional remarks and left.

No, you're quite right — I didn't get the line!

So — if it isn't enough simply to proclaim that you have territory open for which a representative is required, just what kind of a letter *do* you send to the prospective rep? Well, to begin with, of course somehow you're going to have to seek out names of rep firms who are active in your field. How you do this is up to you: admittedly, it may not be too easy. The ways are varied. You might ask for referrals among your fellow sales managers. Trade associations have various ways of transmitting "lines available" information to their members. Trade directories in your industry can be an excellent source for applicable information from which you could select possibilities. If you have been doing business in the territory, some tactful inquiries or requests for suggestions from a few of your better customers might elicit good leads. Your reps in other territories can frequently be a very helpful source for recommendations, since they are very apt to know their contemporaries in various parts of the country. Trade papers carry the ads of reps seeking lines and, of course, you can do your own advertising in such publications.

Before starting your letter to the prospective rep, mull

over the following facts: you're going to contact a marketing authority, a pro in his field and a responsible businessman. In contemplating the addition of a new line to his roster, he has to consider such basic factors as his promotional costs weighed against the potential of the proposed line, that it will involve placing his reputation at stake, that it will draw away a certain amount of the time and effort currently being put forth by himself and his staff in behalf of his present principals. There are many facets of evaluation for a rep to consider in taking on a new line. That is why the terse, generally worded letter like the example given early in this chapter, conveying practically no information on which to base even a tentative opinion, is practically a complete waste.

So now, let's go over the situation in detail, right down to the nitty-gritty of what your letter to the prospective rep should tell him, to include all or a major portion of the following:

Make every effort to select rep firms to contact whose activities seem at least relatively compatible insofar as promoting sale of your products is concerned. (This would seem self-evident, yet many sales managers contact firms based on their size or prominence in the industry rather than the particular fields in which they operate).

Send each rep firm individual, comprehensive letters, preferably addressed to the head of the firm. (It's good psychology for him to learn you have taken the trouble to ascertain who he is, that you are specifically interested in considering him as your possible representative).

Describe your products. You don't have to go on for pages, of course, but supply a reasonable amount of identifying description. Best of all —

really, a must — is to supply your catalog right along with your letter and any other applicable literature available. A few words about your products' main features and how they stack up with competition could be excellent inclusions.

Describe the size of your factory. That you are a small manufacturer is not at all a determining factor, but it does have some significance and, in any case, your prospective rep will want to know this. Such information should include number of employees, plant footage and facilities, how long in business and, very important, identification and background of the ownership.

Indicate what you consider your main marketing category. Do you sell "distributors" or "industrials" (OEM etc.) — or both? Retailers? Or — ? Name some of the well known people in the territory now or previously customers of yours.

What are your commission procedures? Do you follow the pretty much standardized practice of sending out your commission checks in the month following shipment? Or, are you one of those stone age archaics who holds up commission payment until you have been paid by the customer? (Apparently there are still some anachronistic manufacturers who fail to realize or are unconcerned with the fact that the rep has regular overhead to meet, and that he depends on his commission checks to cover his costs of doing business. In a sense, when a manufacturer holds up for an unreasonable length of time the payment of commissions earned and due, he is forcing the rep to help finance his business — and that isn't what a rep is paid to do!)

Do you offer an extra-curricular cash *award or some form of higher commission rate for a special increase in business in some predetermined time?*

Have you been doing business in the territory before, and, if so, who was your last representative and why did you part company? If you still have a rep who is to be terminated, have you notified him of your intentions?

What kind of advertising do you do? Do you exhibit at trade shows? Do you require reps to man your booth at shows?

To what trade associations do you belong?

Do you intend to retain any "house accounts?"

What is your policy with regard to supplying samples?

When you have sales meetings or rep training programs: do you pay all or part of the rep's expenses when attending such sessions? (If you do, for how many of his firm?)

Do you offer any realistic cooperation insofar as costs of pioneering your line are concerned, if it is new and requires an introductory program?

What is your policy when business is built up in one territory with a certain customer, but the order is actually placed in another territory, i.e., that is, what do you do about "split commissions?"

If you have a standardized sales contract of your own, does it provide for reasonable, fair "payoff" to the rep with whom you are parting, based on the period of time in which he has given you representation?

Just try, Mr. Sales Manager, giving your prospective rep *that* kind of information in your initial contact, and see how fast you will get evidence of avid interest in representing you by the best reps in the business! I'm sure you expect to enter into all the foregoing when negotiating with a prospective rep but what should be realized is that if you wait *until* the negotiations *start,* you just aren't likely to get to that point with the more desirable reps. In any event — what's objectionable to giving out explanations of your policies in dealing with your reps? What can you lose?

Then, turnabout — in addition to general suitability, information the prospective rep should supply if interested in your line:

You will want to know the makeup of the rep's firm in detail, i.e., how many of his staff in sales and how many in the office, and does the owner get out in the field to sell or is his function mainly administration?

You should be supplied with at least brief resumes describing the sales people in particular — general experience, technical qualifications, ages, how long in the rep's employ. You certainly have every right to know who these people are who will be using *your* company's name when calling on customers, when they say *they* represent *you.*

Though not going into exact figures, a reasonable question for the rep to answer is how his firm's sales people are compensated — whether by salary or draw, combined with a commission arrangement, perhaps a profit sharing plan or whatever — the justified interest from your standpoint being whether or not these people have enough incentive to work hard, with willingness to stay with the job on a permanent basis. Also — are training programs provided? And do employees as well as owners attend national conventions, factory sales meetings, etc.?

Presumably, the rep's first response described the territory in which he works but it would be interesting to know if he concentrates in favor of one area rather than another, and why. Also, are his accounts specifically broken down among the sales people? If so, is this by sub-territory, or by line? Could arrangements be made permitting you to personally size up all the sales people since it is they who would be representing you in person to the customers?

Does the rep put on special sales promotion programs — such as exhibits for the trade, sales training for distributor employees? How about mail advertising, to be closely followed up by phone and personal calls? Does he maintain mailing lists and are they categorized according to trade divisions? What does he include in mailings? How often are his lists revised? Does he have mechanical facilities for making mailings? Copier? Does he use EDP for forecasting and other such purposes rather than simply for bookkeeping data? Has he TWX or Telex?

What about warehousing? Depending on your kind of merchandising, the possible merits of warehousing on his premises (if he has the facilities) as against in a public warehouse, could be questioned. If he is a "stocking" rep, does he carry the inventory and does he conduct this branch of his activities in his own or under a fictitious name, and how would he feel about your requirements in this respect?

His roster of lines calls for close scrutiny. He should not be reluctant to tell you his overall gross sales volume but, decent business ethics indicate that you don't ask or expect him to reveal the sales volume on any of his lines in particular. However, it is not out of the way to ask which he considers his major lines by way of indicating in what kind of products or markets he is apt to be strongest. In any event, you ought to check with his principals for reference purposes (but telling him beforehand that you intend to do that — does he object?)

A most important point bearing on your future relationship will be what his practices are in making reports to his principals on general conditions or specific situations in his territory. Does he have fixed intervals for these and in what form does he make such reports? If you have definite routines of your own about the contents, length and frequency of such reports, how will he react to the way you want it done?

The single-man rep operation and its merits.

When a sales manager is contemplating the appointment of representation for a given territory, one of his first considerations will be the amount of manpower required to provide

proper coverage. At first glance, the rep firm with the most-
est salesmen would seem the firstest choice. Under some
circumstances, this might be true, but it does not *necessarily*
follow that the larger the rep firm's staff, the greater the
coverage. Other factors make all the difference — one being
the number of lines carried, another the character of lines
represented, and a third the character of trade to whom the
manufacturer is catering.

The advantages of a multi-man rep organization are self-
evident. Coverage! Intensive working of the territory because
of many salesmen available! The services of a "regional"
manager in the form of the firm's head, for which the
manufacturer pays nothing over the usual commission! For a
new manufacturer, the large number of lines carried making
possible the "department store" approach — that is, sales
calls on so many customers, providing numerous opportunities for "suggesting" a line of which the trade might not
otherwise have heard! The responsibility, the prestige of the
large rep firm operation — yes, sure, of course there is much
to be said for the "big" rep company. In all honesty, can one
say otherwise?

Yes, but — otherwise, there *is* much to be said. For
instance: is it likely that *all* of a "big" rep firm's salesmen
work en masse on any one line? Isn't it more plausible that
the lines would be apportioned or divided up among the
firm's salesmen? That's an iffy question! It all depends on the
firm's policies. The point is raised only to remind the sales
manager that the day of the "one man rep" is not yet over.

For the "one-man-and-a-girl" operation, that single man is
likely to be a mature, seasoned salesman, very often a former
sales manager or otherwise more experienced than the younger men ordinarily employed by the large rep company. He is
compelled to limit the number of lines he takes on *because*
he is a one-man operation and so each line is more apt to be
worked in depth. The principals are served capably by a man

who is in business for himself, who is completely dependent
on what he himself produces, who can't just walk out and
hop from one company to another, as the hired hand can and
does — he is totally committed. No getting away from it — he
has *got* to work hard, *got* to make his lines pay off, *got* to do
a good business on the lines he handles because he's *got* to
eat! As a result, the manufacturer placing his lines in the
hands of a one-man operation receives a great concentration
of effort, of intense application to the job. Another point in
favor of the one-man rep is the fact that the sales manager
knows just who it is who will be calling on *his* customers. In
the case of the multi-man operation, it isn't always possible
to meet and become acquainted with the entire rep staff, to
judge just what kind of impression each one makes on the
trade; and of course the sales manager doesn't have the say
about the men who will be facing his customers.

Some feel that the kind of line whose products are bought
by a wide variety of people might be best served by the
multi-man firm, whereas the single-man might be preferable
for lines requiring specialized selling because of the products'
technical nature and prospects to be especially selected rather
than called on at random. Like so many generalities, however, such a rough rule of thumb is immediately broken — for
example, in the case of, say, a line of household wares sold
through distributors, supermarkets or drug sundries trade.
Obviously, a line like that could be serviced by either the
multi-manned or the one man operation.

At any rate, in making the appointment, the sales manager
should keep in mind the *nature* of the one-man operator who
chose to become a manufacturers' representative, remember-
ing that such a man comes with built-in motivation making it
mandatory upon him to get good results for his principals.
One can only repeat; he has no cushioning — no salary
advances, no drawing accounts, no *nothing* but what he earns
by the sweat of his own brow. With due allowance for the

unquestionable advantages of the multi-man coverage, at the
same time the sales manager would do well not to disdain the
"one-man operation" but rather to give much thought to the
possibility of being represented by a man who *has* to do a
good job — or else!

Marry in haste, repent at leisure.

In the final analysis, by way of sizing up your prospective
rep, admittedly nothing beats the eye to eye meeting, if it
can be possibly accomplished. Unfortunately, in so many
cases, this reasoning leads to a sales manager suddenly appear-
ing in town, without preliminaries, to start phoning around,
making it known he is seeking a rep. On the strength of
resulting brief interviews, in finger-snapping time a rep is
appointed and the sales manager flies back to the plant,
hoping he made the right decision.

Manufacturers' representation's most notorious drawback
is the fact that, so often, sales agreements are about as lasting
as a woman's hair "permanent." The kind of representation
arrangement thrown together in a hasty manner is very likely
doomed to be short-lived from the start because insufficient
time was taken to disclose what later turned out to be the
incompatibility of the two parties, such as perhaps personality differences between the rep head and the sales manager.
Impatience of the principal with the apparently slow methods of the rep's start on the line, a misunderstanding about
who is to pay for samples and many other such potential
situations can lead to an early parting of the ways. Exchanges
of correspondence beforehand, leading up to the personal
meeting, verbal discussions and a comprehensive contract can
forestall conditions arising to bring about early severance of
relations.

Just one final word on the subject of attracting the best
reps, having much bearing on the success or failure of a sales
manager's philosophy in dealing with manufacturers' repre

sentatives — namely:

Commission rates vary of course from one industry to another, even within a given industry, but one principle involved is common to all: if, say, the average commission rate in your industry runs around six to eight percent, you are nevertheless going to find reps willing to take your line on at four or five percent — and that indicates just exactly the kind of capability they offer. It's not a matter of a rep giving you a limited amount of service in proportion to the lower commission rate amount. The point is that he isn't *worth* more as a rep or he wouldn't accept an appointment to represent your company at the low rate — you get what you pay for! ☐

VII

WHO OWES WHAT TO WHOM?

A two-way street named "Responsibility," with traffic control by Conscience

A contract purports to include the duties and obligations etc., etc. of the signatory parties. But in the representative-manufacturer relationship, much is *inferred* — far beyond the black-and-white provisions of a written document. A sort of gentlemen's understanding of trade practices supplements the actual contract. Unfortunately this leaves open possibilities for debatable if not actually head-on contradictory interpretations of how the representation agreement's provisions are to be carried out. Let's review some of the responsibilities underlying the written contract, starting with what the rep owes to his principals as he traverses *his* side of this two-way street.

Reps are quick to criticize the sales manager for his alleged shortcomings. Sometimes they are right. Given the widely varying personalities and capabilities of sales managers, it is quite possible the rep may be justified in his criticisms, on one score or another. On the other hand reps, too, are human. There are those who fail to recognize their very real indebtedness to manufacturers. They may fall short of performing in accordance with what the principal has an *inherent* as well as contractual right to expect.

Getting all wrapped up in developing his own future, the rep can become oblivious to how much had to happen in the past from which he was some day to benefit, in which *he* had no part — the early ideas, the designs, the research and development, the trial-and-error period, the financing the years of sweat, toil and accomplishment, the creation of conditions which *now* make it possible for him to *be* the manufacturer's representative. Let us not lose sight of the fact that if it were not for the manufacturer's past, the rep's business would have no present! let alone a future!

Every once in a while, it might not be a bad idea for you and your staff to review just what your obligations are to the manufacturer who has appointed you to represent him in your territory. Briefly recapped, a list could be made up that would go something like this:

> The principal expects you to *know and work your market.* That means not only the current trade that "everybody calls on" but the possible customers in out-of-the-way areas, the new prospects always coming up, studying the trend in products that may affect your principal's current line, knowing the needs coming to light for products that your principal could possibly make, being aware of specialized local conditions of significance . . .
>
> He knows you have other lines but he expects you to spend a *noticeable,* reasonable amount of time working in his behalf. Some product lines are sufficiently well established and popular enough to practically sell themselves. But having such a line, the rep is not privileged to coast, to give it only nominal attention. The sales manager can rightfully demand that you function to increase that popularity, that you keep spending enough time and effort on his line to *earn* your commission . . .
>
> He expects you to keep in good *communication* with him. If he knows *his* business, he won't have

you tied up at your desk, writing endless reports, when you should be out in the field selling. But he does rely on you to keep him informed on what he should know, i.e., the status of an important deal, a significant change in an old customer's purchasing personnel, some new conditions that might affect a customer's credit, the enthusiastic approval of a satisfied customer that could be turned into testimonial use, how the company's pricing is accepted — in short, what *you* would want to know about what goes on in a territory if *you* were the sales manager . . . .

If business is off in volume in your territory long enough to be of concern, the sales manager has a right to an *honest explanation* beyond merely excuses, because only if he knows the facts can steps be taken to attempt rectifying the situation . . . .

He has a right to expect aggressive, self-starting *sales promotion,* those special efforts required to supplement personal calls. Such might include periodical in-house sales meetings, visits to the factory, mail order programs, advertising in various media, holding demonstrations or seminars for the trade, activity in exhibitions and trade shows — and conceivably more, depending on the conditions and variations of your industry.

Well, I'm sure you get the idea. So — how's about it? Are you in good communication with your conscience? Does it have you feeling that *your* performance is beyond reproach?

H'mmmmmm?

The other side of the street

In all good faith, the rep enters into an arrangement to sell a manufacturer's products. And "faith" is the word! The rep has nothing to do with design and production, delivery, with carrying out the routine of properly filling orders. In very few industries does he maintain test facilities; he is in no position to exert quality control. He makes every effort to ascertain the work and performance characteristics of the product to the extent of his technical orientation but, let's face it: ordinarily, he has little more to go on than a sketchy knowledge of what he sells, stemming largely from *what he has been told by the manufacturers*, in one form or another.

It is the manufacturer's responsibility to prove that the rep's faith is not misplaced because the rep's livelihood is directly at stake. The rep must have every reason to be confident that his principal is completely honest with him. Information by inference or in fact that is incorrect or misleading in any sense may, in all innocence, be passed on by the rep to his customers, to reflect on or damage the rep's hard-earned reputation when the true facts become known.

The principal has no right to endanger the rep's standing with the trade. Delivery promises and any conditions relating thereto should be realistic. Statements describing the product's qualifications, applicable data such as precision in weights and measurements, catalog descriptions — in short, all information for the customer must be absolutely dependable insofar as is commercially possible. That is without question a responsibility of the manufacturer to his sales representative, as well as to the ultimate buyer.

Communication! What a cliche word that has become! How many books have been and are still being written on the widely expanded need and art of passing what is in one mind to that of another! But we are concerned here, at the moment, only with the importance of information required by the rep for the customer, and which is a responsibility of the manufacturer.

It goes without saying that the rep should be kept fully supplied with comprehensive literature describing the product and, in applicable cases, where advice and instructions for its proper use are concerned. But what of questions about some particular function of the device, of a specific nature asked about delivery, about errors in billing or delivered quantities and other such questions concerning everyday routine? Why should the rep be put to the cost of expending his time, letters, phone calls and wires, to repeatedly request answers to such matters, to have to keep apologizing to the customer for delays in getting the awaited response, to bear the burden of customer criticism for his apparent neglect of the customer's problems?

The manufacturer employs people and machines to turn out his products. Sometimes one or the other fails. If the rep is expected to act as though a branch of the factory, shouldn't he be made aware of these conditions, of the reasons, so that he can anticipate the customer's reactions by getting ahead of the complaints, by frankly admitting the situation before the customer's anger has been aroused? It is the manufacturer's responsibility to keep his rep informed *in time* for the rep to try and placate and hold the customer's loyalty to the troubled principal before it is too late.

This writer will never forget the grinning sarcasm of an important buyer long waiting for answers to expediting of an order. "I'll just do as I usually do with such suppliers," he snapped, "I'll wire them a cancellation. That will bring back a wire telling me the order was just shipped yesterday!"

There was no disputing the effectiveness of his drastic method. But what about the disparaging effect on the rep, trying so hard to "sell" his principal, and his humiliation in being made to look inconsequential to his customer because of not being able to get reasonably prompt answers to his questions in the customer's behalf?

The manufacturer has a definite responsibility in supporting his rep's efforts and reputation with the trade. One of his most important duties is prompt replies to requests for answers by his reps — and if nothing else, at least an explanation of why the reply has been delayed and when the proper response will be forthcoming.

A matter, perhaps in a gray area but which the manufacturer ought to keep in mind insofar as his responsibility to the rep and the customer are concerned, might be in the instance when price or model changes are in prospect. Should a customer be allowed to place a large order when it is known that prices are shortly to be reduced or that an improved model will replace and perhaps obsolete the number he is buying? Negative! Circumstances will vary widely in this situation but, regardless, the onus for not having advised the trade beforehand certainly should not be placed on the rep! That is the principal's responsibility.

The matter of commissions — when and how paid — can be a sore subject if the manufacturer fails to recognize his responsibility to the rep. We are not referring necessarily to inflation when we speak of the rep's greatly increased costs of doing business. It is fact that expansion of modern industry has brought with it corresponding increases in expenses in the operation of any business, even though an enterprise may be no larger than a two or three man sales office.

Although we long ago outgrew the opprobrious "peddler" as applied to an individual's selling methods, unfortunately all too many manufacturers still think in terms of a rep working out of his home, that he uses the family automobile to make calls and has his wife or kids taking messages for him on their home phone, so that the commission check must be practically all profit. With the possible exception of absolute beginners in the business, that concept is utter nonsense.

Today, the established rep has all the operating costs of office rent, phone and wire communication, secretaries and other office workers, knowledgeable outside salesmen, travel expenses, insurance, social security contributions, bookkeeping and accounting services, advertising, attendance at conventions and seminars, and a host of miscellaneous expenses.

It is sometimes said by the unwitting that the rep business does not require capital, as in the sense of a merchandising business. The hell it doesn't! No less than any of the billion dollar corporations of the country, with their stock issues, their loans from major lending institutions and all that, the manufacturer's sales representative, too, needs money with which to keep his business going. And if he doesn't get it from commissions, where is it to come from?

The point, then, is this: the rep has to meet his obligations right on the nose! The rent has to be paid on the first of the month, the employees exactly on time — he has little or no leeway insofar as paying his bills on the precise due date is concerned. In consequence, the manufacturer who delays sending out the rep's commission check when due is dodging his obligation to the rep working so assiduously in his behalf. It is absolutely the principal's prime responsibility to remit commission checks *periodically on a pre-determined date of the month,* just as he does in paying the wages and salaries of his regular employees, and *no later than the month following shipment.*

I am no lawyer but some years ago, an attorney told me of a principle he said was basic in law, to this effect; that a contract drawn up to all outer appearance in proper legal form, duly signed, witnessed and notarized, could be declared null and void by the courts if it were proved manifestly unfair to one of the parties. One may think in similar terms of the representative-manufacturer sales agreement. In the final analysis, carrying out the provisions of such an agreement fairly, in written fact or implied, becomes the determination of men of good will and conscience. If one of the two parties doesn't do right by the other, it follows that sooner or later their sales agreement is going to become null and void as adjudicated by "termination" or "resignation." □

VIII

MUST I BE THE
CREDIT MAN—TOO?

Yes, Mr. Rep — under some conditions

It is often said that, as a representative or agent, one functions as an arm of the manufacturer. Unfortunately, in so many cases, that's all it amounts to — only those words. But not so to the conscientious, responsible sales rep who realizes that, in effect, for many purposes he **is** the factory in his territory. In consequence, one thing is sure — he is going to see to it that his principals collect whatever money is due for the goods he sells for them. Which is to say: the best way he "sees to it" is **in advance** — by forestalling confrontation with any afterfact payment problems that could arise.

And there are ways and means. It isn't all that difficult or time-consuming.

Of course it's easy to say: "My job is to get the order. That's what I'm paid for. My principal has to have a credit department, receivables manager or some facsimile thereof. That's not my responsibility; it says so in my sales agreement. If they want credit info on the orders I send them, there are national organizations specializing in that business; go get the reports from them and leave me to use my time getting more orders."

Well, technically speaking, you're right. However, there are situations when the man who takes the order, being at the center of the action, might be able to supply better or faster pertinent credit information than that of the people who make a business of it. You are there! You could have been already selling the newly proposed customer, be entirely familiar with his operation, knowing from frequent experience that he is good pay. It is asking a great deal to expect a national credit organization to be that right up-to-the-minute, that intimate with the paying practices of every last individual in business in the United States (with the possible exception of being allowed enough time to come up with special reports).

This is not by way of selling the well known, reputable credit people short or being disdainful of their services — not at all. What I am referring to are the sudden, localized changes that sometimes take place in your own backyard, the time lag between history and current situations, and particularly the possible need for requiring credit information about a brand new account all but within the hour.

Where you come in

Suppose your principal does subscribe to a credit information service (not always the case). But how often can such an organization go through its processes of investigation and formalizing of reports? Yes, improved procedures and especially the computer are shortening up that time lag; but doesn't it still call for time and work of a human being to secure the information intended to be programmed into the computer? So how complete and how recent are their records? How dependable their accuracy?

There can be a gap at which the professionals leave off and the personal touch of the cognizant man on the scene fills in. Above all somewhere, somehow, **somebody** has to attend to checking credit status when you have a desired customer demanding delivery as of yesterday (even though he waited until today to place his order!)

We are not **too** concerned with run-of-the-mill situations or when sufficient time is available for regular, routine investigation of a new account. Where **you** get into the act is (a) when your principal doesn't have access to a commercial credit service and information is required fast or (b) he does, but the data on file is too meager or very old or (c) when you have a principal who, for one reason or another, looks to his territorial representative for immediate, pertinent data or (d) particularly in the event of the unexpected, the unusual situation that may come up.

Which reminds me of the man who returned home from a six-week selling trip. "Anything happen while I was gone?" he asked his wife.

"I'll say! A burglar got into our bedroom!"

"Gosh! Did he get anything?"

"I'll say! I thought he was you!"

In the business world, one does not take things for granted. The alert rep keeps an anticipatory eye out for variations from the norm, including imminent circumstances which might lead to inroads upon his principal's bank account. Take a situation like this, the case of a comparatively new but well regarded firm, whose owner suddenly acquired a luxurious, handsomely appointed yacht. At his "first voyage, open house party," his tongue loosened by many drinks, the host loudly proclaimed the costly boat and everything in it was paid for by cash, he emphasized.

Someone asked, "How did you do it?" The host responded with an elaborate, knowing wink. But it didn't take long before local reps learned, because of rapport previously established with high-placed employees, that the owner had injudiciously withdrawn a significant portion of the company's working capital to pay for his expensive indulgence. Perhaps he was prompted by the stupid assumption that he could justify the expenditure as a "deductible" . . . . That is the kind of timely, on-the-spot information a rep picks up which makes him invaluable in appraising possible difficulties, before his principals get stuck with a bad account.

It is not at all infrequent that the mere fact of being

familiar with what goes on in your territory (as you should be) causes you to be aware of happenings that may plunge a firm into financial trouble. Perhaps you've learned that the customer himself has just suffered disastrous losses — could be one of his own sizable customers going bankrupt, perhaps from a ruinous embezzlement . . . He may have started drinking to excess, to the neglect of his business . . . . Maybe he's become involved in a highly damaging lawsuit; a breakup of principal owners of the business might be in prospect . . . . Might be even a big property settlement divorce suit is in the works . . . . But I'm sure you can visualize any number of exigencies liable to affect a businessman's ability to meet his obligations in proper order.

You've probably read that, in one recent year, ten thousand business failures occurred across the country. That being so, as you become aware of some threatening cloud looming up, is it your duty to forewarn your principals of another possible disaster in the offing? Your conscience gives you a bad time; you're sorry for the man in trouble. But to whom are you beholden? Are you that responsible, conscientious representative or agent, that "arm of the factory"?

Well, my friend, the "lady or the tiger" decision is going to be up to you. The examples given are, of course, hypothetical; but such things have happened. Naturally, it all depends on actual circumstances and calls for the utmost in thoughtful judgment. However, underlying whatever the facts may be, you have to remember that your principals look to you to protect their interests. *That makes* **you** a credit man in your territory.

Sizing up a new account for instant credit

The most common credit question likely to confront the territorial representative is the brand new customer, with whom you have never dealt before, of whose financial circumstances you know nothing, and in particular, who demands immediate delivery — like, right now! from your local warehouse stock or, "Phone the factory and tell 'em to rush my order out today!" That kind!

Suppose, under these circumstances, you have a principal pretty much dependent on the rep for guidance as to which way he should go with regard to shipping open account. It's your ball! How do you go about securing enough information immediately, to be useful in such situations?

The first decision is easy. If for **any** reason the customer refuses to allow enough practical time to check his credit, you'll do well to refuse the order. In all probability, you'll save your factory a credit loss and yourself a commission charge-back — plus wasted time and a lot of headaches. That guy is no different from the stranger proferring a check who grows indignant because he is asked for satisfactory identification.

If the gent acts miffed, is reluctant or evasive in supplying credit information, don't say you haven't been warned! No experienced, legitimate businessman refuses to supply applicable information when asking for or expecting credit from a supplier to whom he is not known. That is, he won't be coy **if he is sound!**

But you are dealing with a new customer who is reasonable and cooperative. To begin with, in the course of your calls on him, you've sized things up. You've seen and heard enough to guess they "should" be okay. You've made it your job to ascertain the number of employees, learned how long they've been in business, let your practiced eye estimate their inventory, observed they are doing a lively business on the floor or by phone, and so on. So far so good. This all has bearing. But you still have only appearances, which could be deceiving.

You may recognize some of the products they stock as being sold by some rep or agent whom you know. Good! Later, that will be one of your first phone calls, when you'll ask your friend how this outfit pays its bills. Could be you know several such cooperative people (**you should have cultivated them beforehand**) who would be willing to exchange credit information with you when the occasion arises.

You request your customer's financial statement and/or at least three trade references with whom he is **currently** dealing (making sure he gives you the key individual's name and exact address if a reference happens to be some nationally widespread corporation with many branches or departments). Your man may greet this request with a short wave of the hand, accompanied by a kind of dismissing, "Oh, you'll find we're rated." That's all very well but persist, telling him that because of his need for speedy delivery it would be faster if he could give you some particular references for immediate contact. **But in any case, regardless of anything, get the name of his bank!** More on that later.

Now back at your office: phone the local references for verification immediately. You may run into a surprising oddity on this score. One or two might say, "Okay with us," while a third comes up with unfavorable information, such as having to wait far beyond stated terms for payment. Still another could respond with similar criticism reflecting on the manner in which the account handles its obligations.

I could never quite figure this out. Did the customer think a salesman, presumably concerned only with making his commission, wouldn't bother checking the given references? Or did he feel that as long as his references said he **did** eventually pay up, the new supplier would be satisfied? I can't explain it, only that I know it does happen that way, and not infrequently.

The customer's bank

Now, for the most important of all: the new account's bank! If he was able to give you the name of an officer there who is familiar with his account, that helps greatly. The official named recognizes the legitimacy of your call on him because you evidently had been told of his familiarity with the client. You just tell the bank who **you** are, that you're seeking credit information on one of their clients who gave them as reference, and why. (Don't leave this function to your secretary — **you** do it. This may not please the women libbers but a male voice is more apt to be accepted as authoritative to the bank official who takes the call and you'll get more willing answers.)

It is difficult to understand why so many people are reluctant to request credit information from this neutral, most significant and, generally, entirely reliable source. Who is better equipped with factual, applicable information? Customs may vary somewhat from one city to another but, in my experience, I rarely had to do anything more than to give the customer's bank a call and, in return, be supplied with such information as to how long they had the subject client's account, his average cash balance (usually phrased as "in the high four figures," "the middle five figures," etc.), what credit experience they have had with him, whether or not he kept up his payments promptly or that he still owed and was paying "satisfactorily" on a loan, sometimes even to how much of a line of credit they would extend to him upon application.

You'll probably be asked how much money is involved in your deal. Chances are they'll follow with an expression of approval. I have had bank officials become quite loquacious, telling me of personal background about the account and the individuals running the firm and going on to state, in so many words, that they consider the client entirely responsible.

I can just see some of you readers snorting with skepticism at the thought of a **stranger** being given so much presumably confidential information **right over the phone** by a bank. Perhaps they shouldn't; I can only tell you that I went through this routine many times and it usually resulted as I just said. Once in a while, a bank might balk at telling me what I wanted to know. (This was more apt to occur when I happened to get some window teller or other lower echelon employee. I learned the best bet was to ask for "a credit officer who would be familiar with the X— Company's account.") But in the rare event of a complete turndown, I would simply call my own bank who, in turn, would get the information for me promptly. Just took longer, that's all. But getting the information at first hand, yourself, is better.

Occasionally, circumstances might have me writing the referenced bank for the information instead of phoning and I would get a response but it would take several days or even longer, and the answers would be brief. I suppose banks hesitate to go out on a limb in writing under such circumstances but verbally they usually proved quite expansive and cooperative in supplying the desired information.

It sometimes developed that the customer's average cash balance was comparatively small — not necessarily a decisive fact although it naturally involved evaluating the significance of this as related to all the other factors entering into the deal. But curiously enough, the possibility of a bank responding with definitely **unfavorable** credit information, as sometimes happened when I called commercial references, just did not occur. Never once did I get answers from a bank casting doubt upon the subject client's honesty and sense of reliability. I could only surmise, it's **different** when a bank is named for a reference. Presumably, the customer would not have offered his bank as a reference if he wasn't very confident they would give him a good send-off!

But don't just take that as conclusive. Contact the bank in any case, especially since, in addition to hard facts, you may get some interesting fringe information from the bank official which will help a great deal not only in sizing up the new account for credit but good to know in your future dealings with him.

And finally, insofar as **your** recommendations are concerned: **don't put your own head on the block.** It's not for **you** to pronounce the account as "good." When you pass along the information you've put together, **quote** the references. Make it plain that you are only repeating **what you were told**, with final judgment up to the **principal.** After all, there is a point at which your responsibility must end.

It may not be much fun making like a credit man, but it's better than having to explain and apologize to your principal for sending in orders that resulted in a credit loss, to say nothing of charge-backs against your commissions! And all it takes to minimize that unpleasant possibility almost down to zero is to ask some commonplace, routine questions, followed by a few phone calls. ☐

IX

MANNING THE BOOTH

Should you?

You have principals exhibiting at one of your industry's trade shows. If your luck isn't too good, you may be afflicted with one or more of those horse-and-buggy age sales managers, the kind who still demand your presence in their booths for periods of hours and sometimes even through all the days the show has to run. Your job? To wait on the people stopping at the booth.

This is a bad deal.* With rare exceptions, it can be taken for granted that the reason the rep gets stuck with booth duty is because the manufacturer can't afford to bring qualified factory personnel to the show — or because he has an over-developed sense of business economy and he can get away with imposing upon his reps. More is involved than the sales manager's indifference to his reps' displeasures. One of the reasons some trade shows are suffering diminishing attendance can be traced to that very practice. These short-sighted ones overlook the fact that *trade visitors don't travel all the way to trade shows for the purpose of talking with reps.*

---

* It is assumed the reader will understand this chapter is not intended to apply to the kind of ballyhoo "Show" put on for retail trade, wherein salesmen might very properly be expected to be in attendance in the booths for the purpose of doing business right then and there, or at least for picking up prospects.

Nowadays, experienced reps very often skip attending trade shows albeit with reluctance. One reason is the feeling of injustice engendered by unthinking or chintzy sales managers. Not only must the rep pay for his transportation and lodging plus all the incidental expenses, which he takes philosophically — that's part of the game — but what he resents is expecting him to stand in the principals' booths, to wait on visitors who in the main are from territories other than the rep's and who consequently mean little or nothing to him. Since he's paying his own way, his right to invest his time as he sees fit should not be encroached upon by sales managers in a position to take advantage of him. Besides, it boomerangs:

Aside from the unfairness of appropriating the rep's time without compensation, what is objectionable about this reps-manning-the-booths practice *from the manufacturers standpoint?* Just this: the trade attending for whom the manufacturer is exhibiting is made up of people who come to meet and talk with *factory personnel* in addition to viewing his products. I've heard purchasing agents say this in just so many words again and again:

"I can see the reps in my own office any old time, night or day, any day of the year! It's *the factory man* I want to see!" He's got problems which he feels are beyond the scope of the rep to solve . . . . He's corresponded or talked over the phone with suppliers — he's curious about them, wants to meet them face to face . . . . He may not think too highly of the rep but wants to maintain or enhance relationships with the manufacturer . . . He'd like to discuss application of a special device proferred to him by the rep which is beyond the rep's technical ability to work out in engineering depth . . . . In short: he's not there to listen to just sales talk. He feels the "factory man" *has* to know more about the manufacturers' products than the reps and his stopping at the booth is for the purpose of learning from this expertise. If the booth attendant, then, turns out to be a rep, he is not only disap-

pointed but, very likely, the rep, bored, has difficulty showing interest in him ("he's not from *my* territory"). The
consequent impressions the visitor gets from stopping at that
booth can result in quite unfavorable reactions.

In addition to the importance of sales meetings with his
principals and visiting nearby factories at convention time,
the rep has many purposes for utilizing his time at the "Big
Show." He studies the show's various exhibits by way of
keeping up with development of the art, particularly scruti-
nizing what competition is presenting, entertains visiting customers, meets and talks with his principals and particularly
their staffs, chats with rep friends from other territories with
whom he exchanges ideas, new methods and various information of interest, picks up customers of his and leads them to
his principals' booths to have factory personnel give them
special attention, and tends to a variety of matters pertinent
to his business.

But there's another side to the booth manning situation.
There are times when the rep *wants* to be there and *does*
belong in a principal's booth. He may realize he needs more
education in the manufacturers' products and in the booth he
can discuss their characteristics with the factory engineers,
superintendents or other top factory personnel able to speak
authoritatively and helpfully to the reps — (*if they were
there!!*) Some questions confronting the booth attendant by
visitors may be entirely new to the rep, not yet brought up in
his own territory. He has an opportunity to learn the answers
himself — the information might come in handy. Customers
from other areas may relate experiences entirely outside of
anything the rep has come across yet and, again, he might
learn something of value. Or, he may be awaiting the visit of
important customers from his territory to whom he wants to
show some particular items on exhibit, perhaps be present to
introduce a key man to the sales manager and make a
flattering fuss over him, and to steer the conversation in

directions which will interest the customer. He may have made appointments with people of significance to whom he has given the principal's exhibition number, using the booth as his temporary show headquarters. But to be or not to be should, in this instance, be up to the rep's own judgment.

There may just be a bit of justification for asking the rep in whose territory the trade show is being staged, to act as a kind of host, to spend more time in the booth than reps from other territories because he is apt to know more of the visitors than anyone else, where to turn for emergency help insofar as packing and shipping of exhibitions is concerned and be better able to assist in case of localized situations. But other than for the special reasons cited, the rep can do much more good for the cause if he isn't tied down to what is pretty apt to be the unfair and probably poorly handled chore of "manning the booth." ☐

X

CALL REPORTS

Working the rep for free work

I was told recently of a manufacturer (unfortunately, there are others like him) who supplies his reps with a special form of his own concoction, for the rep to use in reporting on every call. It instructs him to fill in the customer's name, address and phone number, individual names and departments of all cognizant persons there such as purchasing, engineering and even managerial personnel, along with each one's area of interest and influence. Although one might expect it, somewhat obligingly the form does not require dates of birth, country of origin, nor even call for an oath of citizenship! It does provide a generous amount of space in which the rep is instructed to enter a detailed account of the call, with provisions for additional comments to be made after follow-ups.

One of this manufacturer's reps was overheard describing this encyclopedic form with considerable enthusiasm because, he said, it sets up such a fine, detailed profile of the territory back at the factory. That familiarizes the sales manager with all the various accounts, he gurgled which, consequently, makes possible fast and efficient communication when discussing them — like saving the rep the time of writing lengthy letters. And furthermore, he babbled on, this is how to render real service to one's principal.

Oh, boy! What gullibility! It is suggested to any naive rep who might be similarly minded, so eager to be a Santa Claus, that he would be *really* serving humanity if he were to offer himself to the Salvation Army, to VISTA, to the Peace Corps or to some like worthy cause in need of people willing to donate their services without financial compensation. What a crack in the glass! When you consider how reps invest countless hard, sweating hours, months and years of digging out and accumulating such precious information! Why, this is the rep's stock in trade! That he is duty bound and, in the principal's interests, most properly *should* employ his familiarity with the trade, along with his background experience, goes without saying. That's his job! But that is quite different from being called upon to provide laboriously accumulated, in-depth, detailed files for the factory, as compiled from individual calls.

A rep who gives his all, as per the above referenced sheep so ready to be sheared, has to be pretty shallow in his thinking! Aside from supplying important services without compensation, he doesn't seem to realize that in equipping the sales manager with all that beautiful information, placing it right there at the man's finger tips, he has made it possible for that sales manager to smoothly switch reps at the snap of those fingers to some other fellow who might have become his favorite of the moment, or to a direct factory office if so minded, without having to undergo even a brief break in relationship with the trade.

Another manufacturer of the same ilk likewise demands that his sheep fill out detailed forms covering calls but, along with this states categorically he wants no reports otherwise. That is, he asserts he can judge and sense from these concise notations all he needs to know about what is going on in a territory. He points up, virtuously, how these save the rep's time in relieving him of the necessity for composing special lengthy reports.

This sales manager believes he is qualified to judge what is happening in a territory from terse, formalized reports on each happening. He does not realize it is the rep — the man on the firing line, working in his own back yard become so familiar to him down through the years, who is in the best position to evaluate the results of his calls, to put his summarizing together in meaningful form for his principals *if, as and when circumstances call for it.*

Aside from the arrogance of their demands, such manufacturers overlook at least two pragmatic facts: one is that so many men in commercial life aren't just too facile with the written word. As is frequently demonstrated when it becomes necessary to compose a telegram, a concentration of the right combination of words to convey a message meaningfully, isn't easy. Listen to the average man describing a given situation. Try to estimate how many words and how much repetition he uses to get over what he has in mind: then visualize the same man presenting the subject in a handful of written words. How likely is it for the manufacturer to really get a comprehensive picture of a situation from a form that allows only for short phrasing, limited space fill-ins?

Another fact is that such forms have the effect of reducing the rep to a door-to-door salesman and pencil pusher. Arbitrarily abbreviated reports are not likely to allow for what the rep can offer from his know-how, his brains, what he might supply in the form of suggestions, of constructive criticisms, of special details bearing on a given situation. As just a random example: would a form provide for the case of some personal quirk in a customer's makeup that, as we so frequently encounter, significantly influences his buying attitude?

As may be noticed, this writer makes no bones about being disgusted with those Mickey Mouse mentalities who would keep the rep tied to his desk, scratching his head while he tries to compose some kind of placating words for the sales manager (?) while wishing he could be released, *to be out on the territory,* to be working at his paramount function which is to *produce sales!* If, as and when these demanding sales managers get off *their* duffs and make field trips into the territories to help the rep in person, the results would be much better for their mutual cause.

Or, an increasingly popular and highly intelligent practice is the "rep councils" idea. A selected number of veteran, respected, knowledgeable reps are invited by the factory (at the principal's expense!) to meet with the principal's top people at the factory. The "council" is held in a free exchange of ideas, opinions, criticisms, suggestions. The reps report on field conditions for edification of the principal's people. The manufacturer "tries out" new products, prices or policy changes on the reps. With the feeling of "family" engendered by such get-togethers, the results are bound to be productive.

Then we have the case of the sales manager who demands individual reports, if not on *every* call, at least on those made in connection with the bingo cards or other leads he has passed on to the rep. That guy just doesn't understand manufacturers' representation. If the rep acquiesced in such demands, he would soon have nothing to write about because he'd be using up so much time writing reports there wouldn't be any time left to make enough calls to produce reports! The established, self-respecting rep will not respond to this foolish, unjustified waste of his time. If the sales manager doesn't have confidence that the rep will handle "leads" and calls intelligently, he'd better get himself a new rep. And, in turn, if the rep is going to be pestered with needlessly piling up his paper work, he'd do well to have a very plain understanding with that sales manager on the point or look around for a replacement line.

The sales manager should know that the experienced rep generally has fixed routines for regular work. His day starts usually with going through the morning mail. This probably includes batches of so-called "leads" from principals, consisting of responses to the manufacturers' advertising in the form of coupon requests for catalogs, "bingo" cards out of magazines, along with letters or postcards of enquiry. The experienced rep is well aware of how valuable some of these leads can be. He loses no time culling them through; a lead goes stale very quickly; the enquiry can be forgotten by the time someone contacts the man who mailed it in. (He would wish his principals wouldn't hold these until accumulating a batch, as not all but some do. What a false sense of economy — to pinch pennies on postage in view of the dollars it cost to produce the enquiries! It is only sense for the manufacturers to shoot out the leads to their reps the day they receive them).

At any rate, knowing his trade, the rep can immediately classify the leads. At a glance, he recognizes most of the names of importance or insignificance, as the case might be. He notes the same old requests for catalogs from coupon clippers, such as hobbyists. The batches may include something say, on the order of a hand-written letter requesting prices on single or small quantities of an item ordinarily sold by the gross or in thousands; the rep will see to it that the enquiry is properly taken care of through a distributor or dealer. Of course, catalog requests from perhaps already known or identifiable companies, from major institution librarians, from buyers, from a variety of individuals who have influence on purchasing, are promptly attended to if the manufacturer hasn't already done so; in some instances, such requests can be extremely meaningful to the rep, indicating interest from an important source, to be followed up immediately. Other specific enquiries form another group.

He finally has the leads properly classified, the chaff separated from the wheat. Some are important or promising enough for follow-ups by personal call or by mail. The worthless ones are tossed away. After which, what purpose is to be served by taking up time to tell the sales manager just what was done, what happened or didn't happen in the case of *each* of these alleged "leads," other than or until any of the leads develop particular significance?

Does this indicate disdain for reporting the results of calls to one's principals or the need for keeping them aware of what's doing in the territory? Hell, no! The rep who *doesn't* make timely, applicable reports is not only remiss in his obligations to his principals of keeping them alerted to what goes on in his yard but loses the benefits of the assistance his factory people may be able to give. *However* — such reports should be based on enough information gathered to contribute something toward bringing about a desired result, i.e., orders! If, in the course of a call on a run-of-the-mill customer, the rep is told his pricing is too high when compared to the competition, to waste time reporting such a single call to the factory, detailing this kind of complaint, is pointless. Why should such a commonplace reaction from an insignificant prospective customer be taken seriously? *But* — if the rep gets the same unfavorable complaint resulting from a noticeable *number* of calls, *then* he has something to report, indeed. That is a situation calling for discussion!

If calls reveal that competition is having success with a new product intended to replace one sold heretofore by the rep's principals, if verbal enquiries about a particular device indicate the possibility of a new market opening up, if significant conditions in the territory change in one way or another, indeed yes — the rep very definitely should be making summarized reports of territory changes and developments to his principals and welcoming their comments or advice.

Of course, it may be taken for granted that there will be exceptional situations. Certainly extreme circumstances may arise of a critical nature wherein the rep needs every last bit of help he can get. In such a case, he will place at the disposal of the factory all the applicable data available needed to use in working on the situation. But ordinarily, in the usual course of things, it comes down to this, with analogous situations leading to the same conclusions: the sales manager will appoint a rep with a hearty "Good luck — now get out there and bring me business," based on the assumption that he has acquired the services of a *professional.*

Such a rep, expert in the selling field, will undoubtedly maintain an organized, comprehensive call report system* in some form or other, with all the detail, and the follow-ups and the whole thing, as required for his sales promotion and miscellaneous activities of his business. But while this costly, arduously acquired information is used in behalf of his principal, it has been and will continue to be accumulated on his own time, so to speak. A major part of a rep's value to his principal stems from intimate knowledge of his territory. It is foolish to belittle and weaken his position by permitting himself to become the dog-like expedient of a dictatorial sales manager's "go, fetch and carry" policy. It is the judgment brought to bear by the rep in supplying adequate, properly informative feedback and the extent to which he complies when he has to contend with time-consuming, short-sighted sales managers, that separates the self-respecting, independent professional marketing specialist from the ordinary salesman. *Anybody* might be expected to have some common sense but it's the application of *uncommon* sense that denotes the superior man!

Before leaving this subject, I must tell you of one such never-to-be-forgotten sales manager whose demands called for all but daily reports from me (disregarded!) who, in one ludicrous happening, got upset because a certain, very important prospective customer wouldn't respond to his request for a report on his product:

---

* REF. Chapter II of "The Manufacturers' Representative."

Out of my early inexperience, not yet knowing any better, I was devoting tremendous promotion to a very intriguing device but which, in its novel design pattern, differed completely from the part it was intended to replace. In consequence, to use it meant a complete re-design of the customer's equipment, normally a very costly procedure. Besides, to employ it in a new product, would make its manufacturer "sole source" because standard versions of the device could not be used to replace it — obviously, a hazardous position in which the customer would be placed. Despite the interest the component aroused, the going was rough.

(A moment to digress: this incident emphasized an important lesson, namely, to wit, to think carefully before taking on representation of a one-product, highly specialized line. It absorbs disproportionate time and effort promoting the single items, rarely to pay off profitably.) But, back to the story:

As you probably know, in California, we have a couple of prestigious, world famous scientific laboratories who, under university auspices, engage in highly important national projects. The nature of their work is such that rarely, if ever, is it publicized. When these labs don't manufacture themselves, they will farm out sub-contracts, specifying which components are to be used in the finished product. That naturally makes them a regular port of call for reps trying to have their brands qualified for future use.

The trouble started when I asked my sales manager to submit samples to one of these labs but not to look for direct results. I explained the institution's procedures, that whatever they approved might be used by their sub-contractors but that no orders would come from the lab itself. I specifically stated this being a very special situation, the samples were to be submitted only with the understanding that the likelihood of hearing any results would be at some distant future time, that I was staying on top of the situation and would keep him advised if, as and when anything interesting developed.

He apparently understood and agreed because he sent the samples. (In money, the cost of the items figured only in cents per each.) I had given him the name of the cognizant buyer there in order that the samples be delivered to the right people, but I made the mistake of mentioning one or two names of top scientists identified with the project for which the referenced item might be suitable, my thinking only to impress my guy with the stature of this lab.

Within a couple of weeks he started! He wrote letters directly not only to the buyer but to the scientists I had mentioned! He wanted to know what they thought of his device. He wrote again — and again, and again! Receiving no response, with each letter his tone grew more exasperated. As I read the copies of his letters, I tried vainly to shut him up but, no, he continued. I tried to tell him that their silence was not, as he was now stating, "insulting in being so disregardful," that in an institution where Nobel prize winners were so numerous they fell all over each other, he'd better stop trying to get "Good Housekeeping" reports from such people, but he couldn't be satisfied.

Some time later, when I was attending a convention and talked with this sales manager, he actually brought up, in great indignation, the fact that the referenced laboratory had never done him the courtesy of replying to his letters! When I reminded him the samples were requested by me and submitted with that understanding, it was as though I had not spoken!

Of course, that is an extreme example. There were other times, later on, when I had occasion to resign lines without finding it necessary to use the kind of language with which I finally penetrated this fellow's consciousness, but I can only say that it takes all kinds to make the world, and b'golly, when it comes to sales managers, they're all here!   □

XI

ON DECIDING TO BECOME A STOCKING REP

Keeping store is different from ringing doorbells

More and more manufacturers' representatives are going in for stocking merchandise. Whether or not to follow suit can be a difficult decision to make. You've seen examples of reps who have themselves turned to carrying stock for resale and who, as a result, have built up highly successful merchandising operations. But you've also heard of some very experienced reps who tried it and fell on their faces, in all too many cases due to naivete, to not knowing what they were getting into. You are right to be dubious. Stocking your lines can work out most unhappily for the best of salesmen — because that's what, all too often, they are — salesmen, not *merchants*! The rep should know that when he goes in for carrying merchandise for resale, no matter where he physically houses the stock, *he is keeping store,* and that takes a kind of know-how entirely different from solicting business by ringing doorbells.

To be a bit more formal about it: for a manufacturers' representative considering the regular stocking of merchandise for resale, it is imperative that he realize this activity has him functioning as a *distributor,* regardless of what nomenclature he uses to describe the operation. He is urged to ponder deeply on the factors entering into the carrying on of such an enterprise, they being so different and involving so much greater detail than the procedures of calling on trade as a manufacturer's representative.

But now — your decision is made to get into it; presumably you will continue to act as the rep on the lines to be stocked. In that case, the very first thing to do is to work up a comprehensive contract covering the arrangements with principals, they now becoming your *suppliers*. Don't take any definite steps without formal agreements! Don't rely on just a letter. Set up a contract approved by your attorney, one which will anticipate the innumerable questions bound to arise. Right there, you can save yourself many a grievous experience.

So, let's ask those questions!

Since the stock itself forms the basis of this enterprise, we'll start with the inventory: who owns what? Are you going to take title or is the stock consigned? Do you or does the factory do the billing, the collecting? Are bad debts (write-offs) charges against you or the supplier? Who pays the taxes on it? The fire and burglary insurance? The storage (warehousing) charges? Write out the applicable details in your contract!

How often will the stock be physically counted? Will computer read-outs be used? What form for taking the inventory is agreed upon — yours or the principal's? How will shortages be adjusted?

When you take an order, what conditions govern whether or not it is to be shipped from your local stock or from the factory? And what is the price differential between shipping from the two sources?

What about territory? Are you permitted to operate outside of your rep territory? What will your position be with regard to others, the so-

called "regular" distributors who stock the same line: Is there a possibility of your falling afoul of the Robison-Patman Act, of being charged with "unfair advantage" because you have the commission edge in addition to the distributor discount?

Do you have exclusive rights to the sale of the manufacturer's products in your territory? Can he (or you) appoint other rep-distributors in addition to yourself? Have a clear understanding and write it out!

Who gets the referral leads from the principal which he has received from his advertising — you or the "other" distributors?

Do you have protection in the event of price changes? What are its terms?

Have you spelled out a firm understanding about whether or not you can sell other lines? How about "other" lines that are competitive — are you permitted or forbidden to stock such? Write it out!

Suppose you want to "adjust" your inventory — meaning, return some products because of being overstocked, obsolescent or otherwise non-salable. Do you have return privileges? If so, are there time or quantity limits and what will be the penalty charge, if any, for making such "adjustment"? Write out the details!

What will the manufacturer supply in the way of catalog material, samples or demonstrators? If you have to pay for such, what will be the basis for your cost?

What is the time period for which the contract remains valid? Assuming either party can terminate the arrangement, how much notice is required?

Does the contract specifically include the provision that you are not the agent of the manufacturer but are an independent contractor, as is always advisable in rep contracts?

Is provision made for disputes by arbitration?

Does the manufacturer's guarantee or warranty fully and unquestionably establish his responsibility for the performance of his products, specifically absolving you from any responsibility in this respect? Write it out!

Preceding such points, presumably you have given consideration to the basic questions: if you are going to run the operation yourself, can your rep business spare you or survive without you? Will your rep activities be affected by customers looking upon you as a competitor? If you are going to hire help, what is the going rate for suitable employees? Can you afford it? Have you estimated what your overhead is going to be and then added fifty percent to your estimate because it will probably go that high, whether you see it in the beginning or not? The discount to distributors looks huge when compared to your commission rate but how much will be left in the till when you've finished paying every bill?

Life is full of hazards. Every time you draw a breath (air pollution), walk across the street (oncoming truck), sleep on a water bed (drowning) — you're confronted 24 hours a day with something demonically liable to do you in, so don't be discouraged by the foreboding inferences of warnings to watch yourself. After all, the business of stocking lines, as so many have proved, can be particularly rewarding in the way of tangible resources accumulated, as contrasted to the ephemeral qualities of "good will," that last named being about the sum and substance of the rep's "inventory." It's just that what we have been discussing is that, as a stocking rep, you're in a very special kind of ball game, played by rules which should be clear and agreed to by all concerned. Don't rely on simple letters of appointment or verbal understandings. Consider the many possible contingencies and "write it out!"   □

XII

VISITING YOUR FACTORIES

Why should you?

There is no such thing as knowing too much about the manufacturers you represent and the products you are selling for him. The more familiarity with your offerings exhibited, the greater the impression in your favor exerted upon the prospective customer. What the factory people tell you by phone, mail and in your office, and what you see of their catalogs and other literature, is all very well but *seeing and hearing for yourself* while visiting the manufacturer's plant, can be of tremendous assistance when you're back in the field.

At the factory you see the wheels revolving in the principal's offices. You observe *how* and *who* handles the routine — to stand you in good stead afterwards when you need to go to the right person for action. You may learn for yourself where the bottlenecks occur in the handling of orders; you'll know what, if anything, can be done to improve the situation or, if you must, how to allow for it. Your understanding of people will enable you to determine who has and who hasn't clout among the personnel, with the consequent effect on you. You'll perhaps become aware of special relationships between individuals which may influence the course of their business — for example, a nephew of the head man being groomed for a top position, a discovery which would then enter into your acceptance of the younger man's importance in your future.

In the plant itself, aside from general education, you will pick up priceless bits of information, some to fit beautifully into your sales talk afterwards. I once represented a company that started in business by buying certain items from manufacturers which they packaged under their own brand name. Volume grew until, in time, having outgrown being a "packaging house," they were doing the actual manufacturing themselves. Nevertheless, they just could not live down the humble conditions under which they had started and buyers continued to make snide remarks and look down upon them.

On a visit to their factory, I saw many of the items actually being manufactured, and in huge quantities. When I returned to my customers, in talking about this principal, I made much of the fact that I had seen the manufacturing process going on *with my own eyes*. Coming from an eyewitness, and one whom they knew, the buyers were impressed. Thereafter disparaging attitudes about who was making the products for this principal ceased, at least in my territory.

In the case of an electronics manufacturer making a form of semiconductors for very critical applications, the operators at one row of benches all wore white cotton gloves. Carried to this extreme seemed beyond reasonable needs for cleanliness — but it was for the very critical purpose of preventing possible contamination of these sensitive products from the fingers' natural oil. Customers told this simple little fact seemed to be more impressed by it than evidence of the device's electronic efficiency! Well, maybe that's a bit exaggerated, but it *is* an example of how, by some such off-beat interpolation among your prosaic sales facts, you can intrigue the interest of your customer.

There is no need to dwell on the highly important but self-evident advantages of being able to make points for yourself by socializing with your principals as well as learning more about what kind of people they are. But the main thing is your indoctrination in details which might not otherwise be called to your attention. You'll be told things which the sales manager, in his visits out your way, didn't think of bringing up. Talking with this one or that one of the personnel, you'll hear stories of what other reps have come up with in the way of new ideas or methods, which you can apply in your territory. You'll learn of uses for the products which hadn't been brought out before.

The education you get by making visits to your factories is most valuable but, above all, the greatest return is that if *you* find yourself being impressed by the evidences of care, of skills, of efficiency of the factory, by the sincere desire of its personnel to do well by people, you'll carry back with you vibes that will somehow be transmitted to and felt by the customer. If *you* admire your factory, subconsciously, as well as by calculated effort, your convictions will go a long ways toward creating a similar state of mind in the people you call on! You will have become an infectious carrier of good will!

□

XIII

SO WHAT'S NEW?

One of the business world's two most effective words

A man responded to an ad offering a horse for sale. He looked the animal over, then offered $200 for it. The owner refused, insisting on his $250 advertised price. The offer was raised to $210 and again turned down, but the owner dropped his asking price to $240. This back-and-forth continued during the better part of an hour of fierce haggling. Finally a compromise was reached at $225, with the seller agreeing to deliver the horse — and the deal was made.

The erstwhile owner led the horse into a trailer, hitched it to his car and asked, "Where to?" The buyer said, "Just turn that corner there — I'll show you." They drove across town, the buyer directing, until they came into one of the city's exclusive residential districts. In front of an ornate apartment house, the horse's new owner ordered the other to stop. The seller looked at him questioningly.

"We'll take the horse through there," he replied, pointing to a narrow space between the apartment house and the next building. They squeezed through to the back and there got the horse on to a freight elevator, rising to the fourth floor. Emerg-

ing, the horse was led down the corridor to an apartment door, which was then opened by the man who had bought the horse.

"This is where I live," he said. "Bring him in."

The erstwhile owner of the horse stared in disbelief but the buyer motioned impatiently to get going. The door opening having been intended only wide enough to admit people, made it necessary to push and shove to force the beast's huge body through, with the strained jambs giving off alarming cracking noises.

"In here," the new owner said, opening the bathroom door. Again, after a struggle, the horse was shoved through. "Into the tub," he ordered. It was a difficult feat but somehow they managed to get the horse's four legs over the bathtub's edge. "Excuse me a minute," he said, leaving to return a moment later with a revolver in his hand. Raising the gun to the horse's head, he pulled the trigger. The shot killed the animal. With that, he led the horse's former owner to the door.

At the doorway, the startled, open mouthed man who had sold the horse, turned back to his customer. "What the hell is this?" he demanded. "First, you beat my head in, chiseling me down on the price of the horse. Then you have me deliver it to an apartment — everyone knows you can't keep a horse in a place like this. We almost wrecked the doorway getting the horse in and I all but got a hernia, helping shove him into the bathtub. Then — after all that — you shoot him dead! Are you nuts?"

The man shook his head grimly. "Now that it's done, I'll tell you. I've shared this apartment with a friend of mine for the past five years. I get home from the office a few minutes before he does.

> *Every night, when he comes through that door —*
> *again and again, every single night, without excep-*
> *tion, seven nights a week, three hundred and sixty*
> *five nights a year, he never changes, he always*
> *walks in with the same question — 'What's new?'*
>   *"Tonight, by God, I'm going to tell him what's*
> *new — there's a dead horse in the bathtub!"*

Well, it may be, as the French saying has it, "that the more
it changes, the more it stays the same" — that there is
nothing new under the sun, that it may have been necessary
to contrive some such esoteric presentation as the one just
related in order to bring the annoyance of repetitious, cliche
questioning to a halt. But one thing is for sure — the very
word NEW is in itself one of the two most powerful tools
used in business for taking advantage of people's never-ending
interest in the different, the unique, the novel, the modernis-
tic or whatever the guise may be that represents change,
something other than the known.

Its use for commercial purposes dates back to the beginning of barter. From the time of the ancient Phoenicians and
Carthaginian traders up into the space age, with the exception only of "price," nothing is equal in effectiveness, in
catching the attention of possible customers, comparable to
the whetting, the stimulus of the word, "NEW." The world
of commerce is continually replenished by innovation, the
introduction of products or systems different or improved
but always sparked by the adjective, "NEW." Semantically
old though its usage may be, it's a word that has never worn
out its ability to invoke interest.

As such, "NEW" is a valuable adjunct of the rep business.
Many possible uses for it are available, not necessarily involving anything so dramatic as pointing prospective customers to
a dead horse in the bathtub. More conventional methods can
be employed, such as issuing publicity upon acquiring a *new*
line, devising various means of promoting a *new* product,

publicizing and distributing a *new* catalog, that you're moving into a *new* location, hiring a *new* man — and so on. No matter what may be your presentation, never lose an opportunity to make primary, prominent use of the word "new." It grabs for attention!

Your NEWSpaper

In my previous book, "The Manufacturers' Representative," I suggested one way of combating the tedium, the monotony of endless work would be to single out a particular line to feature for a given period, presenting it as "the line of the month." The idea was to give the selected line particular and unusual promotion, creating a contest atmosphere for the firm's staff, offering prizes for an increase in sales volume and for bringing in new customers.

As part of such a program, periodically issuing "NEWS" to the trade can become an important adjunct — or, of course, it can be considered a separate project of its own. Such a publication can take many forms — as, a single sheet or a folded brochure or whatever. It depends on how elaborate you care to make it. You can do the "make-ready" in your own office by pasting up pictures and typed captions, along with descriptive copy, all of which can be readily and inexpensively reproduced by the now commonplace photocopy "instant printing" process. A variation might be to make your "News" look like a newspaper. Since the printing would be done on actual newsprint paper, which is cheap stuff, the cost should be reasonable.

For such a house organ, a catchy title is highly desirable, including a terminology which specifically infers it is devoted to things which are new. That you will have to contrive to suit your circumstances, but it should be something on the order of "Rep's Product of the Month" or "The Monthly Rep-O-Graph" — a good twist being to somehow play on your own name for Rep." The contents should feature one or more outstanding products from the line but always start with announcement of a NEW line or a NEW product or anything else you can hang the word "new" on.

Don't try to make a catalog out of it. Put too much in it and it won't be read. Tell 'em WHAT'S NEW (a possible part of a title in itself). Select timely pictures and or drawings and use these freely — better than a thousand words.

Incidentally, aside from new product description, you have innumerable other happenings to draw on that you can feature. Your firm was awarded a plaque for some record-breaking feat. You have added a new man to your staff, whose background is such-and-such, and who will be doing so-and-so. You were impressed by some particular trade show, quoting statistics about attendance, number of exhibitors, perhaps excerpts from the famous personality who made the show's opening speech. You have just received a supply of XYZ catalogs, available to the reader upon request. Your trade association put on or is planning a meeting to feature an important speaker, a golf or bowling tournament, or whatever. You or one of your staff has become an officer of your association, has entered into some civic program, has become a member of a trade committee. The local Chamber of Commerce announces population growth figures, a predicted increase in business, plans for a new railroad crossing, a drive for new members. A member of your firm has become a father; another might be celebrating the anniversary of a long-time wedding. You are planning a sales seminar for your customers or attended one staged by your principal.

In short: what do you talk about when you're just socializing with business associates? Those are the kind of subjects to consider for your "REP NEWS."

Not to belabor the subject but study the multi-million dollar copy of the big national advertisers and just note how, in one way or another, they feature new *in what they have to sell. You would do well to use the same time-tried and true principle in promoting your business.* □

XIV

CONCENTRATION ON THE CONSEQUENTIAL

The make-ready for the sales call

If you are one of those who, in making your calls, plays the sales interview by ear, it is not (one may hope!) apathy in taking the trouble to be prepared but, most likely, because you don't want to present a monotonously memorized sales talk to your prospect. You know that if you make like a phonograph, he's likely to turn the switch off on you. But in the attempt to be lively, to give the sales pitch spontaneity, you can get started on some minor subject, some trivial matter. The conversation then can become a prolonged back-and-forth between you and your prospect, using up valuable time which should be devoted to the main points you wanted to make.

The professional knows he should anticipate and be prepared before the call to make the significant points with his prospect. So, having dutifully studied the literature or the product itself, he sallies forth to make his calls. But lack of order, jumping about between salient points of the sales talk, can be confusing. And, if the presentation isn't sequentially organized, it becomes exceedingly difficult to keep the conversation moving in the right direction that will result in an order.

How "organized"? First, get together a list of the product's most impressive features, in the order that you think will keep each point in relationship to the one brought out before, to be followed by the rest of its qualifications. (Price?

A good salesman will leave that for the last if he possibly can, unless his product is one sold *primarily* on the basis of price).

In making this compilation of features, *write them out* in order of importance. Read the list over enough times to feel assured you will remember all the points, but being careful not to memorize a *speech*. Better yet — and, highly to be recommended — address your sales story into a mike, recording the features in their proper sequence. Then, listen to yourself several times. (Also — could be — that when you hear yourself as others do, you might want to make at least some changes in your presentation.)

But to what purpose, this chore of making a *graphic* list of your product's features? Because that *special extra effort* fixes the points in your mind and in best order so that, when the time comes to start talking to your prospect, without necessarily sounding like a parrot you will be bringing out the *important* points you want to make before you are diverted or sidetracked into trivia. In other words, after you have gone through the usual amenities, you will be all but impelled to start right in on the first of the features you want to drive home; your memory will then carry you along in the order you had *pre-determined*.

There are those who will feel it isn't necessary to bother writing out such lists, that their memories are good enough to retain all the salient points of what they have to sell. Well — my point is that for one reason or another, *anyone* may somehow overlook bringing forth some telling feature — as in the case of that renowned architect who designed an elaborate, beautiful, two-story house but omitted the stairway. To go to the extent of specifically *writing out the list of points beforehand* is simply a way of making a mental recording, one which will reinforce your memory to guard against the possibility of omitting some significant portion of your presentation to the prospects.

*　　　*　　　*

Polly want an order?

I once had a voluble salesman whose reports about his calls were exceptionally detailed, setting out just what he said to the prospect — how he introduced the subject, how he described the product in all its features, how he compared it to competition, and so on until he had to stop for breath. He always had much to quote of what he had said but little about the prospect other than that, in what was getting to be too many cases, he had been ultimately turned down when it came to getting the order. With such comprehensive presentations of the sales story, it was hard to understand why he wasn't bringing in the business.

Finally, I went along with him on some of his calls, just to listen (one of the experiences that led me previously to urging executives to accompany their salesmen on calls at random intervals. How it pays off!). What I heard in this instance was quite revealing. I learned why my guy was so vague about personal reactions of the prospect or what kind of man he was, bringing back only the fact that the buyer was negative about giving us the order. In each case, he picked up nothing of what the prospect's interests might be, his background, his hobbies, if he had a sense of humor to which one might cater, what plans his company might have for him in expansion or other changes in their business — just nothing about the prospect to which one might orient presentations, no information on which to prepare follow-up appeals to counteract an initially negative attitude. The explanation was simple: my hot-shot salesman never learned anything about the prospect because he just didn't stop talking! I could have sent the buyer a casette sales talk recording; it would have done just as well as his parrot-like spiel.

Over-enthusiasm is like too much sugar in your coffee

Salesmen who are self-defeating are those who, in effect, might as well be really deaf without knowing it because they don't stop talking long enough to become aware of what they don't hear. So many talk themselves out of business because of their verbosity. I'm not referring necessarily to egotists like the big lummox I was referring to above. Nor do I mean the garrulous fellow who habitually runs over at the mouth — the one who is obviously hopeless.

I'm speaking of the over-enthused salesman, the one who becomes *too wrapped up in his selling talk,* that man who, being sincerely overcome with admiration of the product he's offering, non-stops on telling his prospect every last tiny little detail and, repeating himself, continues to talk all the way out to the point of boredom. It is possible to become so sincerely and completely sold up oneself that you simply over-ride and all but disregard listening for and evaluating what the prospect has to say. Surprisingly enough, the fault is common among men who should know better.

Not to bore you with repetition but here, again, is one of the best adjuncts one can apply to help make a proper presentation, and that is the recording of your sales pitch — just for your own edification. When you play it back, aside from smoothing out or rearranging what you have to say, you can make mental note of logical places to stop long enough to let your prospect speak, to create breaks for encouraging him to talk by asking questions related to what you've already said. Those breaks not only keep him attentive but guide you as to his thinking so that you, in turn can judge what more you should say and about what — and to let you know *when you have said enough.*

In all the didactics of how to sell, we have always drilled into us the need for knowing our products thoroughly, for developing that confidence in them which, in turn, we will presumably transmit to our prospects. No one can argue with this basic philosophy of the salesman's presentation. As is proper, presenting one's cause with enthusiasm is all very well but it's like spicing your food — there's a point you reach when enough is enough. And — looking at another angle of it

— in this noise-polluted, uproarious, loud-mouthed world, the novelty of quiet spoken, mannerly, low pressure salesmanship could turn out to be surprisingly effective — such being so different! ☐

XV

A WAY OF MAKING UP YOUR MIND

Thinking via arithmetic

One of our most common cliches, a catchword we use continually, is derived from the punch line of a classic story that I'd like to relate here because it has so much bearing on a predicament in which we often find ourselves:

This Bill meant well, was even likable, but he just wasn't bright. A simpleton, a slow-witted character, he couldn't hold a job over twenty-four hours. His family had become sick and tired of supporting him.

One day a relative came along with, "I've got just the job for you. It's so simple, even you can handle it." He took the docile, willing Bill to a produce market where he was shown a wagon load of potatoes that had to be unloaded into three bins. "You put the big potatoes into the first bin," Bill was instructed. "Then the medium size go into the second bin and the small potatoes into the third bin. That's all there is to it — okay?"

"Got it," said Bill. "This I can do."

So, they left him to his work. Returning at the end of the day, they looked into the bins, to count with dismay only three potatoes in the first bin, one in the second and two small potatoes in the third — the full results of a day's work! They

> *looked around for Bill, to find him stretched out*
> *flat on the ground, glassy-eyed, his face swollen*
> *purple, his breathing all but stopped.*
>
> *"For heaven's sake," they stormed, "what's hap-*
> *pened? Why can't you handle such an easy thing as*
> *unloading those three sizes of potatoes into their*
> *bins?"*
>
> *Bill choked and fought for air, struggling to get*
> *the words out. His croaking could barely be heard.*
> *"It's — it's the decisions," he gasped. "They're*
> *killin' me!"*

Each of us has his own mental procedures for tackling a given problem. Some pitch right into it, others procrastinate but whatever your habits, sooner or later decisions have to be made. And they're not always easy, especially if the nature of the problem is such that only you can solve it.

I'm a great believer in *writing it out.* I've heard about those super-duper minds, those people with the ability to concentrate, to travel a mental path as though it were an uninterrupted freeway, to arrive directly at the requisite goal. But there must be others, like this writer, who don't have such automated minds. We need some form of assistance, a way of organizing our free-floating thoughts, in rounding them up for application to our problems so that we may be guided to the solutions.

One way to do it is with pencil and paper, wherein one uses what I have termed the "value percentage" method of arriving at a decision. To serve as an example, let's take a question common at one time or another to most reps: a national industry convention or trade show to be held in a distant city. The question: should you attend or not? You're having trouble making up your mind. So — try this:

Enumerate every last pro and con you can possible think of that applies to the question by *writing them out* as fast as they come to mind — the pros on the left and the cons on the right side of the sheet, separated by a line drawn down through the middle. Then, give each point a "value percentage" — a figure intended to show its *proportionate* importance in arriving at the ultimate decision. Don't try to be too precise — if you do, you'll be hung up longer than it takes to get to the trade show and return. Suppose it goes something like this:

PRO	CON
One of my principals is holding a formal sales meeting. Not a major line with me, but might learn how to improve it **15%**	*Time element: preparation for the trip, the several days at the convention, the week or two of catching up with the workpile after return.* **25%**
All my sales managers will be there. No specially important matters to take up but a number of routine subjects could be worth discussing **15%**	*Cost of transportation, food and lodging; incidental costs* **20%**
Social get-togethers with my principals — good for helping cement factory relationships **15%**	*Possibility of something going wrong during my absence* **5%**
Sales Managers always like to see their reps at trade shows **5%**	*Possibility of losing out on some good order because of not being on the job* **5%**
Meet rep friends from other territories; exchange ideas and methods **15%**	*So boring — same old stuff — I've been through it so many times* **10%**
New lines possibilities **20%**	
Competitors' exhibits help give me more of a line on what they are offering **10%**	
95%	**65%**

Note that as you write out each point, you are arriving at the comparative importance of each one in graphic, definite form with these "percentage valuations." Then, of course, you add up and make your decision based on the comparative totals.

Once you have tried this method, you will get the feeling of your thoughts being channeled, all but *forced* to concentrate on *point by point* because of the orderly arrangement required and the physical act of *writing it out*. The ultimate effect is to get you off the hook of uncertainty by reducing your problem to a simple mathematical calculation.   □

XVI

THE REP MIGHT TAKE ON A WEAK LINE

It depends

One of the toughest problems confronting the small, little-known manufacturer operating with limited capital, seeking professional country-wide sales coverage, arises when he tries to enlist the services of sales representatives willing to invest time and effort, reputation, their own money, on working the line. Manufacturers and representatives need each other but somehow the rep's objections to taking on a line obviously weak from his point of view, must be overcome if the rapprochement is to be accomplished. It can be done but it takes special conditions, particularly some deviations from the ordinary on the part of the manufacturer.

You are a comparatively new manufacturer, as yet a small and little known factor in your product category. You've put in your years learning the know-how of the business, you're considered an authority in your field, know what the trade buys. You get together with one or two others and pool your savings, add perhaps borrowed money, to market a series of products you've developed which your experience tells you should be salable. You've done a certain amount of market research, you've studied the competition and are convinced that your quality and pricing compare favorably. In fact, between you and your fellow workers, you've already created some interest in your offerings and have even gotten an encouraging scattering of orders.

Things look promising. All you need now is to let all the possible customers know you exist. Of course, you don't have much money for advertising programs. Likewise, your capital is too limited for you to hire salesmen. But the trade doesn't know your company and your products — it's a big country — how are you going to introduce your line in all the possible areas? You and your partners can only do so much — you need a force of salesmen to cover the country. How and where do you get them?

Easy, someone says. No problem. Just put the line in the hands of the manufacturers' representatives of this industry. They operate without requiring direct pay in the form of salaries. You don't even have to pay a cent of their expenses. They go out on their own; if, as and when they get orders for you, you pay them a commission.

Sure, you know about reps. You remember when they used to call on . . . . Yup, that's the way to go. So, you obtain a list of reps, you select the names of those you'd like to have representing your company, contacting especially the more prominent firms, and you offer them your line — on the usual commission basis, the way you understand they work. Result? One by one, they turn you down! Some observe the amenities and send you polite "thanks but no, thanks" notes, others don't even respond to you. You're taken aback, baffled. What's wrong? What does it take to interest a rep firm in taking your line on? *Everybody* doesn't start big. What is it with these reps?

You're a manufacturers' representative. You've got a pretty fair roster of lines but, of course, you're always interested in the possibilities of new lines. You know that, barring miracles, "big" lines don't just fall in your lap but you also know that sometimes the so-called "little" lines can be sleepers. You've heard tell stories of fantastic successes originating from one-time unknown sources so you're always on the alert, paying close attention when you hear of a new line available. Along comes this "XYZ Mfg.," a new manufacturer, only in business a year or so. Outstanding new products — they look salable. Competitively priced, too; the ownership seems to have know-how insofar as the manufacturing and attractiveness of their products is concerned and, as individuals, appear to be quite personable. The field they are entering is not too crowded. The line might be a good bet you're thinking, yet you tell them, "No — thank you." Why? Because you're an experienced rep! You've been there before and you've had it — right up to here!

This outfit? They don't have strong financing. For one thing, they can't afford the kind of advertising that would at least familiarize the trade with their name, help break the ground for you. They won't be exhibiting at shows, at least not for a long time to come, because of the costs. All the load of putting the line on the map will be borne by those reps who undertake its representation. But — unknown lines worked out in some cases for the reps, and very profitably, at that; you know that. Is lack of lots of capital the sole reason for refusing to represent them? No! It's a reason, it is a handicap, but it is one of the lesser objections to turning the line down. If that were the only drawback — !

Aside from any other pros or cons likely to cause the rep's negative reaction are *unfavorable sales agreement conditions.* The subject manufacturer has learned what the average commission rates are in the industry for his product category and so that's what he is offering — blandly or ignorantly bypassing consideration of the extra special time, expertise, hard work and actual money which the rep has to expend in introducing and promoting a new line. It will take months and months at best before the line begins to produce even nominal amounts of commission, it promising to be a long time before the commissions start compensating him for his pioneering efforts.

But even worse: the manufacturer has drawn up a common

type of sales agreement with a termination clause that provides the agreement can be cancelled upon thirty days, perhaps (so big hearted!) sixty days notice! That's a stopper!
Before reps learned better, again and again a rep would be
attracted to a promising line. He'd take it on, give it hard
drive, in time he'd have the line going well. Eventually it
would start proving profitable and, just about the time when
he was beginning to reap some rewards for his work, to at
least recover some of his initial costs in introducing the line —
blooey! he'd be cancelled!

The reason for terminating him? Could be any one of
many. The market now being well defined and a steady list of
customers built up, the manufacturer might feel that instead
of paying a rep so much money in commissions for only a
portion of his time, he can hire a direct factory salesman for
the same amount or even less and get his services on a full
eight hours a day basis. There might be a change in sales
managership, with the new official indifferent to the rep's
early work, preferring to replace the original rep with some
favorite of his own. A huge order might be in prospect and,
to avoid paying the large commission that would be forthcoming, the manufacturer terminates the rep before the deal
is finalized. The manufacturer might enter into a merger or
sell out to a conglomerate and, when it was all settled, the
rep would find himself out in the cold. And so on. All these
examples and more could be cited of the rep getting the
shaft; these are from life. Can you blame him for being
skittish when it comes to taking on a new manufacturer's
line?

So — we have a gap which, somehow, in the interests of
both parties, should be bridged. Each needs the other. How
do you bring them together while protecting the legitimate
interests involved?

In the main, it's up to the manufacturer. How? Well, there
are possibilities if the line has real potential. Assume he is

unable to finance extensive advertising campaigns but that he can at least provide good descriptive literature plus perhaps and, in some way to be worked out, can cooperate with the rep in mailing programs. In a first approach to the problem, the manufacturer does something like this:

1. He is going to have to understand that more is expected of him in addition to just being willing to fill orders. He must be aware that the rep has to be at least partially reimbursed in some way or other for carrying the load, for getting the line started. As evidence of willingness to do his part, the manufacturer might be willing to sacrifice his profit on whatever business the rep brings in within a stated period — which might be, perhaps, one year. For example, offer to pay the rep on the basis of 33-1/3% of the selling price on all orders brought in — as contrasted with perhaps a regular prevailing commission rate of 7%. In other words, assuming the products were really salable, this might help the rep recover some of his pioneering costs in getting the line on its way. The agreement would provide that after the end of the stated introductory period, the commission rate would then drop to whatever was normal in the industry for such products . . . . This isn't the best of arrangements but, in some cases, it might prove feasible.

2. Another and perhaps more favorable format would be that the sales contract include a firm provision giving the rep all the selling rights for a minimum period of five or at least three years. The intent, obviously, would be to protect the rep from being cheated of his just rewards for taking the line on and building it up from nothing. By the same token, protection for the manufacturer from tying up the line with a rep failing to do much with it could be accomplished by setting out an agreed volume of business to keep the contract in force. The extent to which a manufacturer would object to making the sales agreement cover a long period, would be something of a measure revealing his sincerity and intent to do the right thing from the rep's point of view.

3. As against the foregoing, a different approach to the problem would be paying the commission rate considered fairly standard in the industry. Meeting any rightful objection the manufacturer might have to a termination notice period running into years would be simply for the manufacturer to pay the rep a nominal monthly amount for his services in establishing the line. This might be (again hypothetical) say, several hundred dollars per month — or whatever figure the rep would bring up based on his costs of doing business and sufficiently compensatory to permit him to apply all his expertise to give of his time and promotional efforts toward building up the line.

Obviously, such an arrangement is subject to individual conditions and circumstances beyond our scope here but the principle of a guaranteed "fee" to the rep for his initial efforts should offer practical possibilities for meeting the needs of both the manufacturer and the sales representative.

Of course, along with the financing problems of launching a new manufacturing enterprise, runs concurrently the prospective manufacturer's needs for his personal living finances. Well, not to be callous or hard-hearted about it but, nevertheless, that's *his* problem. At any rate, he should understand why the rep has to say regretfully "No, thank you" when it comes to repping *his* line.   □

XVII

ABOUT THAT MONEY-LOSING LINE

When do you quit?

You used every bit of judgment you have before taking on representation of that line. The manufacturer has a good personal background — not in business for himself very long but seemed to know what he was doing; his past activities include lots of experience in the upper echelons of major manufacturers. You became very interested in his products, they being most intriguing, intended to supplant a kind in popular use. Competition is strongly entrenched but he has manufacturing know-how, quality and reasonable pricing to offer, and everybody has to start somewhere. You like him and his staff. At the time you took the line on, everything looked "Go!" In this case, the sales agreement is traditional in that you entered into the deal under the usual straight commission arrangements, with no special compensation. You thought it worth giving a try.

In the first six months you sold almost nothing of this line but, then, it takes time to break in; everybody knows that. After all, the competition is long established and pretty strong. In the next few months, you picked up a few orders; from them you developed some repetitive accounts, but otherwise nothing exciting happened. Another six months — commissions come in regularly now but in small amounts, hardly totaling enough to mean much — yes, true, but this factory — such nice guys, always obliging, willing to cooperate in whatever you ask if they are able to do so. No, they haven't the finances to engage in enough advertising to rival the established brands *but*, if things work out, next year they'll go in for some *real* advertising. Yes, the lack of a good catalog makes it difficult but those individual sheets give the necessary information, don't they? No, they're not exhibiting at the BIG SHOW this year but, next year, just watch!

So, a year of such rationalizing passes, and a second year with this line still in your roster is under way. You've made a very real investment in time and money promoting it with practically no return. But now you've relaxed. You don't work the line hard any more — what's the use? You do have those few customers on it whom you take care of. That the line still costs a share of the general overhead, that it does require at least routine attention, doesn't strike you as very important. You guess the few bucks it brings in ought to take care of that.

Until, comes the day when your apathy and procrastination, your lack of foresight and reluctance to face the facts and do what you *should* do, bursts upon you. How? Well, this is just one of several ways it might have happened: you learn one of the subject manufacturer's strong competitors had found it necessary to make a change of reps; since they knew you already had such a line, of course they didn't contact you‚and somebody else picked up a beautiful line. You all but break a leg kicking yourself.

But much more probable is being turned down on some highly desirable line because the sales manager feels that yours is a full roster, that you already have all you can possibly handle with your present manpower. You begin to wonder how many sales managers seeking representation passed you up on that account.

You wake up! Sadly, regretfully but, finally wiser, you resign the line. You sigh — such nice guys; you wish you could have done more for them. Maybe — it sometimes works out that way — the next rep will take the line over and, with

some other approach, may do very well with it. You hope so
— but you yourself can't keep on losing money on a line.
You make a resolution — to apply what you learned — that
hereafter you will be hard-nosed, that you won't just hang on
to a line based on ethereal promises and expectations, that it
had better show very real returns within a reasonable amount
of time, or you drop it.

The foregoing hypothetical recountal is only a personal-
ized presentation to point up a very common type of potentially harmful procrastination among reps, namely the reluctance to give up a line that is bringing in a few bucks and
doesn't seem to take up any time to speak of. Can be a very
sad delusion! First, although this is the lesser side of the evils
wrought by carrying a poorly paying line, close study will
show that it *does* cost money to retain. You *do* have to go
through all the bookkeeping routine with it, just the same as
is required for your better lines. You do have to spend some
time with him when one of the factory's men is in town. You
do engage in at least some occasional back-and-forth confer-
ences and correspondence with the principal and you do have
your time taken up occasionally by some one or more customers — all this perhaps not often but can come at bad
moments, when your attention is more importantly required
elsewhere. In short: if you will be honest with yourself, a
little thought will prove up that, in one way or another, it
does cost you to continue carrying the subject line.

But by far the worst effect of dragging along a poorly
paying line is, as previously indicated, the fact that it swells
your list of principals. First, if a *big* line of similar products
becomes available, it won't be offered to you, naturally,
because you already have a presumably competitive line. In
any event, foremost in a prospective sales manager's mind is
the question of how much time you are going to or *can* spend
on *his* line if he were to place it with you. When he counts
the number of manufacturers you represent, *he* doesn't con-

sider and isn't likely to accept your explanation that you don't spend much time on that weak line we've been talking about. To him, that's just one more manufacturer whom you represent — and, conceivably, could strike him as just one too many.

So, how now? Take a good, close look. Bring your figures up to date. Right now — does your roster need combing out? Are you handicapping yourself with one or two weak, just so-so lines, perhaps cluttering up the possibility of acquiring a line that could be making you real money? Isn't it plain now that you are just nowhere if you are going to postpone the chopping off process until *after* a desirable line shows up in sight?

Take a good look at your roster of lines and ask yourself: *isn't pruning of a tree at times necessary in order that it grow bigger and better?*   ☐

XVIII

AGENT VS. MANUFACTURERS' REPRESENTATIVE

What you don't know can hurt you

The curious lack of concern exhibited by industry in commonly using the word "agent" to identify the independent professional salesman, presumably indicates unawareness of some of its hazardous implications. And, in view of the locution's established, widespread acceptance, it would be a highly controversial and certainly gargantuan task indeed, to undertake persuading people to abandon the use of the word "agent," replacing it by "representative." (Although there are those, nevertheless, such as in the electronic industry, who long ago judiciously discontinued describing sales representatives as "agents" in favor of "sales representative" or some facsimile thereof.)

In any event, the rep should at least understand the inherent unfavorable and even perhaps dangerous possibilities embodied in use of the word "agent." Surely, when your attorney draws up a sales agreement for you and includes the categorical provision that the rep is *not* an agent of the manufacturer, *as he will* unless particularly instructed otherwise, he must have cogent reasons. *He* knows the legal inferences of the word "agent" and he wants to protect you from its misapplication.

Where the problem starts is that, in the business world particularly, repeated misusage of a word or phrase leads eventually to passive approval and acceptance. An instance is the plainly contradictory expression, "I could care less" — a positive assertion with an entirely negative meaning. Then there is, "You're too much," a deploring negation which, strangely in reverse, is intended to convey approbation or praise. Solecisms like these defy direct conversion into proper English — they always lose something in the transposition. To the pedantic, these unconscionable instances of abusing our beautiful language amount to nothing less than atrocious anti-semanticism.

Be that as it may, these somewhat light-hearted examples of verbiology were chosen in order to point up a similar but in this case very serious paradox poised in use of the word "agent" which, apparently innocuous, nevertheless contains the possibilities of unanticipated legal entanglements, far removed from the user's intentions.

Why should this certainly commonplace, widely understood and generally accepted occupational description be a matter of serious concern to a manufacturers' sales representative? For openers: one lesser but nevertheless thoughtworthy answer may be found in the Random House Dictionary, which offers for "agent" as its very first definition: "A person authorized by another to act on his behalf: *'my agent has power to sign my name.'*" Sic! The example cited is the direct antithesis of a provision incorporated in most formal sales agreement contracts stating specifically the representative is *not* authorized to obligate the principal without special permission or instructions!

A number of definitions follow, but not until the eighth meaning ascribed to "agent" does the dictionary get around to the definition offered as, "a representative of a business." Then, too, note that the first definition infers the "agent" is regarded as one who functions with specific powers and designated duties, as in the case of an employee subject to a superior's dictum, i.e., his employer. Were that the case, it could perhaps make the principal responsible for his "agent's" acts in the same sense as for the actions of his actual employees. In turn, the "agent" might be considered responsible for his principal's acts and that, sir, is why you had better fasten your seat belt!

What this boils down to is that it is necessary to avoid, by inference or otherwise, any possibility of assuming that the principal has control over the rep in a sense resembling his control over employees. Just the commonplace incident of a principal passing on a lead to you which he wants followed up, must be handled without any appearance of you being *ordered* to take care of the matter. You must remember that in the event of litigation, it's how the *courts* interpret the words, which is not *necessarily* how a routine procedure is commonly and informally accepted in one's industry. (As an aside to this very point: counsel for the Electronic Representatives Association advises its members "that representatives not enter into agreement with their principals giving their principals the right to 'control and direct' if the representatives do not want to be subject to a possibility of having income tax withheld from their commissions.")

The significance of making it clear that neither the principal nor the representative is the "agent" of the other, nor should the rep be known by that word, is pointed up in a recent Government publication issued by the "Small Business Administration" entitled "Manufacturers' Sales Representative." In an excellent recap of what a rep is by John C. Warren, consultant and president of Albee-Campbell, New York, the statement is made, "He (the rep) cannot obligate his principals in any way without prior approval. Thus, he is not an 'agent' in the strict sense of the word."

From one industry through another, the occupational descriptive terms seems to vary with the industry, despite the fact that the individual functions may be pretty much the same. For example, in the very forward electronic industry,

practically every sales agreement (as it should in all properly
drawn contracts) contains an unmistakable, sharply worded
provision specifically stating the two parties (i.e., the representative and the manufacturer) *are not agents of each other*,
stressing that the representative is an independent contractor,
with supplementary wording to establish their complete *legal
independence of each other.**

One of the most pertinent reasons for questioning the
safety of using the word "agent" is the growing prevalence of
product liability lawsuits. The recently enacted Consumer
Product Safety Act, its title self-explanatory, may be expected to produce a flood of litigation. You may consider
yourself far removed in relation to a product ultimately
purchased by a consumer, but courts have attributed liability
to *anyone in the chain of distribution,* in terms of the
manufacturer, the distributor, the retailer and the manufacturers' sales agent. Note this, too: in the event of a damage
lawsuit stemming from a happening in your territory, based
on the products of a manufacturer who is in poor shape
financially and who may take refuge in bankruptcy, it could
turn out that *you* are the only one in sight from whom
damages might be recovered if you were legally his "agent."
(Furthermore, it is not only the limitation of your interest in
your own corporation that is at stake — they can go after you
and your personal assets as well. Your attorney can give you
some enlightening information on this last mentioned but so
frequently misunderstood point!)

In a typical property damage liability insurance policy,
among a well known, major insurance company's exclusions
from the policy appears the precise statement that *no responsibility was assumed by the company for* "failure of the
insured's products . . . to meet the level of performance,

----

* REF: "The Manufacturers' Representative" Chapter 14

quality, fitness or durability warranted or represented by the named insured." What the *sales rep* should have is the straight-out assurance that the principal *is* responsible and on the other hand, likewise specifically, that the rep, like the insurance company's disclaimer, is *not* responsible for the manufacturers' performance in any respect.

Thinking in terms of the unexpected liability that can happen: I was once told of a ludicrous incident resulting when a plumber was confronted with the job of overhauling a malfunctioning water heater in an otherwise well preserved old Victorian mansion, the home of one of the city's leading families. The lady of the house, bound by sentiment, nostalgically refused to have the aged contraption replaced by a modern heater. Fix it, she ordered.

The old style heater's intricacies proving too much for the plumber, by special arrangement with the heater manufacturers' local representative, he sent it back for repair to the still-in-business factory, installing a temporary heater for the interim. After a prolonged wait, the equipment was returned, completely overhauled, now presumably in good working order. Pressured by his customer to rush it up because of a big party she was putting on that night, the plumber worked overtime with the unfamiliar equipment but finally got the water heater installed and operating just before the festivities started. Soon thereafter, one of the lady guests retired to the guest bathroom. Suddenly a piercing scream emanated from the bathroom. Everybody rushed to the scene, to find the lady writhing on the floor in great pain.

Someone had made an awful mistake! The water lines to the toilet had become crossed in such a manner that when the lady flushed it, an unexpected torrent of scalding hot water was released, instead of the usual cold . . .! Though unable to sit down for a long time thereafter, eventually the lady recovered but, in the meantime, everybody in sight was sued — the host, the plumber, the factory and its local "agent."

The incident was related to me by an insurance man (his company having taken over and settled the damage suit) to illustrate the fact that, far-fetched though it may appear at first, in *addition* to the principal's assurances, a sales representative should have insurance to cover the contingencies to which he might be exposed. These hazards will vary somewhat from one industry to another but all will probably have in common the damaging possibilities of malfunctioning products, the chance that delivery of an order wasn't made as promised and therefore the customer suffered deadline penalties, or perhaps a shipment ordered was short or the wrong goods shipped or arrived damaged and the manufacturer disclaims responsibility, or warranties and guarantees weren't being carried out to the customer's satisfaction who then resorted to the courts — and other dire potentials pertinent to your industry that could lay your head on the block, which you and your insurance man should discuss.

Certainly, when it is all said and done, product liability insurance is a must but, preceding that, as I have said so many times: when negotiating a line, submit the sales agreement to your attorney before you sign up, making sure it includes a provision specifically absolving you from all responsibility for the performance or promises of the principal. That may not be 100% conclusive (is anything certain in this world, besides death and taxes?) but it will go a long ways toward protecting you — just in case — with a good insurance policy as your final backup.

As for changing from the ambivalence of "agent" to "representative" at this late date: your own circumstances will have to govern your course. Probably continued acceptance of the subject word is a pragmatic conclusion because of the tremendous difficulties involved in getting away from its long established usage by the public as well as the trade. However,

if you have a choice, "representative" is absolutely the pre-
ferred word. In any event, protect yourself by the responsibility provision in your sales agreements and by a well
thought out product liability insurance policy.   □

XIX

GOOD WILL

Who are you?

Like the personality from which it stems, it's intangible. You spend years of effort and untold sums building it, in ways and means beyond count. It has pervasive presence but without body. Means of acquiring it take many forms, some apparently quite ordinary, yet having much bearing on earning the trade's favor. While difficult to place a monetary value on it so that ordinarily one lists it as an item in inventory at one dollar, "good will" is nevertheless your most valuable asset.

Arthur Brisbane, the one-time famous columnist, used to say, "If it doesn't pay to advertise your business, advertise it for sale." Still true — but aside from advertising you pay for, there is a kind of advertising available which is effective and, better yet, costs nothing. That is what we euphemistically call "publicity" in its various ways and means, i.e., getting your name into print. When well cultivated, it becomes a part of that all-important "good will" in that it helps create your "image."

Desirable publicity involves playing up events indicating progress, achievements, triumphs. Issue "p.r." on moving to new quarters, an addition to your staff, a years-in-business anniversary celebration, an award in observation of a record-breaking feat, a company picnic, the acquisition of a new line, a prophecy of business increase next year — any happening that you can seize upon as an excuse for a "press release." You've been reading these things in trade publications yourself, in the business and financial pages of newspapers about others. You will do well to follow suit. Such "news" has a subliminal way of impressing people, as shows up in the case of meeting a prospective sales manager who, to your gratification says, "Yes, I've heard of you" — which harks back to having read some of those publicity items about you.

Be sure to have a supply of *good* portrait photos of yourself on hand to accompany your "p.r." — taken by a professional photographer who is told the prints will be used for commercial publications, rather than the soft versions for home exhibit (so that he will make them sharply detailed, contrasty, on glossy paper). Very often, the availability of your picture will decide the editor on whether or not to run the item about you.

And another thing: for heaven's sake, if the nature of your occupation isn't a secret, see that it gets tied in with your name. From time to time, I receive many letters in connection with my writing or other projects, so that I see examples of letterhead in the scores. I am simply amazed to note how many businessmen (which is what I have to *guess* they are!) neglect to show who and what they are in business life. A name, address and a phone number — period — that's all the letterhead shows in a good many cases, not even including the words "Manufacturers' Representative." Don't you think it important to give yourself identity? Does your name bring on a "Tom-who?" reaction?

There are those who shyly do include some wording admitting that they are, indeed, manufacturers' representatives, but they don't specify in what industry! It is estimated there are 400,000 manufacturers in this country! Is simply your name, as one of them, going to be meaningful in a business sense?

How can one overlook the advertising value (i.e., helping to build good will) of telling people what your business *is* whenever you have occasion to write a letter? Does it cost any more for your letterhead to help make you known to the people to whom you write — or to those among whom your letter may be distributed, for one reason or another, who never heard of you?

And while I am on the subject of letterhead, although I wrote about this previously in "The Manufacturers' Representative," it is important enough to repeat because so often neglected in otherwise well designed stationery: don't forget to show logos on your letterhead of any major organizations to which you belong and, if you've been in business a lengthy period of time, show the date your company was established. Such indications of solidity, of responsibility, do just that much more toward enhancing that "good will" we were talking about.

Incidentally — about stationery — usually the company name is shown big enough but I just don't understand the absurdity of permitting essential data (i.e., address, phone number, etc.) to be be printed in characters so small that they require hard squinting in order to decipher them — in some cases too difficult to determine what they are *even with the aid of glasses.* If the rep deals with youngsters who probably still have keen vision, this may not be critical. But if your trade consists of people in, let us say, from the thirties on into the later years (deep sigh!), you will have customers who, confronted with printed matter, reach into their pockets for reading glasses, if they don't already wear bifocals.

Dr. Carl Kupfer, Director of the National Eye Institute, is quoted as saying, "About one hundred million people wear glasses." With that kind of widespread eye-weakness evident, I should think it would be obvious that people ought not be unnecessarily irritated by stationery with the imprinting too fine to be read easily. One may well remember the truism: the easier you make things for your prospects, the more likely they are to become and remain your customers.

In this case, simply select type large enough to be read comfortably by people of average eyesight but not obtrusive enough to call attention to itself because of its size. There is such a thing as swaying too far the other way. Every so often, I see an example of a gaudy, hugely spread out logo and accompanying data sprawled across the page to take up perhaps a third of the usual 8½ by 11 letterhead, looming up like a veritable bullboard! One tends to recoil, to back away from the overwhelming blatancy of the personality it betrays. Admittedly — there is a place for showmanship — there are industries where flamboyancy is entirely in keeping and to be expected — but these are few and far between.

Reminds me of long bygone years in Los Angeles, when cynical Easterners, decrying the fantastic growth claims emblazoned across the firmament by the real estate men of those days, chuckled that the contrived word "realtor" must have stemmed from the local Spanish influence. (In Spanish, "real" means royal and "toro" means bull!) One may ask, gazing at the incredible megalopolis centered about Los Angeles today, how many of those comics who may still be alive rue the sense of humor that obscured their visions of the future!

The beautiful gesture — to make it and to spoil it

As a "good willer," in "The Manufacturers' Representative" I described the idea of phoning a customer *after* the transaction was *entirely* concluded, to ask if everything had turned out all right, to ascertain whether or not the buyer was fully satisfied with the manner in which his requirements had been handled. It's a gesture that can be sensational in engendering good will. Reps who tried it found customers were delighted at the interest exhibited since the rep, having presumably received his commission, might well have been assumed to have forgotten the customer and the whole thing — a wow as a good will builder-upper!

Unfortunately, some reps missed the point, failing to realize that the good will value was embodied in sincerity, that the rep had to be honestly concerned in following up after the transaction was concluded. If the rep really doesn't care, the phoniness of his supposed interest is bound to show and the procedure will do more harm than good. But aside from that, specifically I am referring to reps who, after enquiring and being told the customer was satisfied with the goods and service, didn't let it go at that but went on into a sales pitch about another line or product. The good will effect of the phone call was immediately destroyed.

Today's sophisticated public knows that selling by phone is common, that sales people use all kinds of dodges to hook the attention of the person being called. In this case, the customer jumps to the conclusion that the rep's enquiries about the customer's satisfaction were only hypocritical, that in fact the rep was simply using a ploy to get into the real purpose of the phone call, i.e., a sales pitch.

I can only repeat: to really get the benefit of this "Thank you — how'd we do by you?" phone call, limit it strictly to what it purports to be — that you want to be sure the order this customer gave you was properly handled, the product proved as represented and the service satisfactory. Then, after the customer has expressed himself, unless *he* initiates a question about something else you may be selling (quite possible), *hang up* with some pleasant "Be seein' you — take care" type of sign-off.

Then — with the realization of the excellent impression you have made on this customer, and feeling confident you will be well received *at some later date*, you contact him for the frank purpose of making your sales talk about whatever it is you want to get into with him. Doing it that way, it is my bet that you'll bat out a thousand per cent more attention and consideration.

It is evident that you're not going to phone *every* customer after the transaction is through and over with, just to express a continuation of your interest in him, that you desire to know the service you rendered turned out well. Naturally, you'll be selective, probably going to this extent only with your more important customers.

However, by way of fully utilizing this idea, it is suggested that you consider *a letter* to each customer for the same purpose. Start it by thanking him for the business. Ask if the order he gave you was completed to his entire satisfaction, that if not you want to know, that you are concerned about your customers, that you want your trade to realize your interest doesn't stop with delivery of the merchandise. Wind up with some wording urging that you be personally called if everything wasn't hunky-dory, and sign off with an expression of appreciation for his business.

A letter isn't *quite* as good as the personal call but, it can do lots of good nevertheless, worthwhile enough to write it widespread to just about every customer of any consequence at all. (But — for the same reason just cited — don't speak of other products.)

Still another unusual gesture would be in the case of a transaction handled by one of your salesmen. A nice touch is to write the customer thanking him for the business he gave your salesman and expressing your personal interest in knowing that everything was handled to the customer's satisfaction. The point here is the feeling of trust created, the confidence of dealing with your firm that it instills in your customer, to know he is being cared about by the *owner* of the business, that *you* are aware of his existence. It speaks well to him for giving you his business in the future.

The company name — should you use your personal name?

The individualist character of the rep philosophy naturally incorporates a desire to establish one's own name — given and surname. Reps seldom adopt such company names as, "General," "Standard," "Ace" etc. It's always like "Joe Soandso," "John Rep & Associates," with very few looking ahead to the significance of names of a general type — de-personalized identity being just the opposite of most reps' intentions.

The point is not at all critical until comes the day when, by whatever course is followed, you step out of ownership of the business which has been operating under your personal name. You sell out, you retire — in any event, you're no longer in command. The business goes on under your name BUT *you* are no longer there to guide its policies, to continue the methods that established your reputation with the trade.

After you're out, though still in your name, profound changes are bound to follow. They may or may not be to your liking and perhaps you will no longer care — unless, as sometimes happens, your successors deem it necessary to belittle you in order to enhance their own stature. What if they are generally inept or their practices bring into disrepute the name you labored so hard to build up for so many years? What could you do about a disgruntled customer, rightfully or wrongfully, speaking caustically of the firm by *your* name? Wouldn't that make you squirm?

Or: suppose the firm is well known, long established under your personal name and you take in a partner. You are now confronted with changing the company name, bringing the new man's name into it. It will take a long time and cost considerable before the trade's confusion over your company name is cleared away — the publicizing, costs of registration, legal papers notices, expensive changes in letterhead, business cards and so on — much of which would be unnecessary if your firm had been known by some impersonalized name as, say, "General Sales Co." Also, there is the employee who either by specified arrangement or his hopes, looks forward to owning an interest in the business or, even more likely, it may be a matter of his ego but, for one reason or another, perhaps subconsciously, he resents the use of *another man's name* identifying the business to which *his* time and *his* effort are devoted, the inferiority implications perhaps to engender resentment.

Still another point — frequently disproved and minor, but worth thinking about — is that a firm known by *a* man's surname sounds small; whereas, a fictitious, *big sounding* company name is more impressive. And the intangibility of manufacturers' representation is such that anything contributing to impressions, no matter how minor, has greater impact than in a merchandising business.

About that fictitious name

In considering the adoption of a fictitious name (and applicable to your own name, for that matter), try it out on strangers *over the phone* before making your final decision. No need to enter into technical discussion here of sound characteristics but, suffice to say, we know that some sounds are more easily misunderstood than others — and vice versa. It is not only an irritating nuisance to keep repeating who your company is, but in addition, it seems to work out that if people on the other end of the phone have difficulty understanding the company name, it extends to being unable to remember it readily in the future.

Study the phonetics of your proposed name. George Eastman considered this when he coined the word "Kodak," making sure not only that the word did not exist anywhere in the world but that it could be pronounced clearly in any language. Something of the importance and value attached to a company name may be visualized when one contemplates the fact that according to one of their stockholder reports, bringing the Standard Oil Company of New Jersey and affiliate companies together under the one name "Exxon," was estimated to have cost them one hundred million dollars!

And yet we list good will in inventory at one dollar!

*   *   *

Would you like to be assured of multi-million-dollar success in building a huge corporation, but enough to become a national byword? It's very simple, really! All you need to do is to coin a company name that will include the letter "x" and limit it, preferably, to two syllables. You would then be following in the footsteps of such as Timex, Purex, Cutex, Rolex, Kotex, Syntex, Tintex, Playtex, Kleenex, Purex, Pentax, Borax, Onyx, Exxon, Exlax, Clorox, Bendix, Textron, Xerox, Dextrose, Windex, Chemex, Telex, Pyrex, Silex, Kardex, Trendex — whoosh! You take it from there!   □

XX

TRADE ASSOCIATIONS AND THE CAVE MAN

The lone wolf belongs back with the dinosaurs

In one sense, it is possible for the overly independent spirit, carried to extreme, to be a major handicap for the rep laboring to reach the pinnacles of success, just as would be the case if he were trying to climb a steep mountain by himself. Today, cooperation with the majority in his industry is mandatory if the rep is to make progress; the lone wolf in business life has become an anachronism.

An accepted indication of maturity and accountable performance to be expected in an industry — an instance of professionalism, if you will — is the existence of a well organized, active trade association. Membership in such organizations in itself marks the individual firm as one of responsibility. And an industry group working in unison for a common cause, by virtue of numbers, if nothing else, is able to bring about important advantages for its respective members unlikely to be achieved in any other way.

What are these advantages? The range is wide — slight, perhaps, when confined to a group merely meeting for luncheon or dinner, whose purpose hardly extends beyond the social, the "steak-and-potato-club" type of thing — or it may extend into a long list of extremely worthwhile benefits. Active associations can include most if not all of the following for its members:

INSURANCE — *Associations can receive the benefit of low cost group rates on every form of insurance.*

DIRECTORIES — *Pro-rating among the members makes it possible to produce comprehensive, fully detailed directories describing the individual firms for minor cost — a service to be highly valued by the trade.*

DISCOUNTS — *Car rentals, auto and battery purchases, hotel and motel rates and other items become available at substantial discount to association members.*

CREDIT — *Ratings and experiences with delinquent or unscrupulous manufacturers can be recorded at the association's head office, to be available to the members.*

NEW LINES — *Lists of lines available can be accumulated for dissemination among the members. The association's publications can be a central source of advertising by principals or reps.*

NATIONAL SHOWS — *The association can put on its own "conference" or can attend trade shows officially, there to promote the interests of its members.*

HOUSE ORGAN — *Magazines, other publications and trade news can be issued of interest to the members.*

SEMINARS — *Arrangements can be made with leading universities to put on training programs and "work shops," keyed to the members' interests.*

FINANCIAL SURVEYS — *Data can be gathered from all members for compilation to create meaningful average figures for the trade.*

CONTRACTS — *Suggestions for model sales arrangements can be drawn up for the members to follow and to urge upon principals.*

LOBBYING — *Selected individuals can be arranged for to represent the industry's legitimate interests in Washington.*

IMAGE — *Membership in a trade association can be publicized to enhance the individual firm's standing in the trade.*

COOPERATION — *When members break bread with their fellow reps at association meetings, valued friendships and good ethics can develop. Timely, informative speaker guests are available for meetings, pertinent films can be shown, members can exchange ideas, experiences, credit status of accounts, changes in territory personnel and other bits of information worth noting.*

The list of advantages can be extended even further or varied to fit the individual requirements of the association. Current examples of two trade associations very active in behalf of their rep members are the "Manufacturers' Agents National Association" (MANA) and the "Electronic Representatives Association" (ERA). MANA is an old established, highly respected association, welcoming reps from all industries, whose benefits include all the foregoing listed and others. As a one-industry association, ERA is a prestigious organization, carrying considerable weight in its industry and offering all the benefits listed; however, membership is confined to reps established in the electronic industry.

For reps in special occupations where trade associations do not exist, who recognize the potential advantages in prospect of banding together, the expenditure of some effort in getting an association under way need not be too difficult, as might appear at first glance. Mainly and basically, it calls for a couple of dedicated individuals — two or three men willing and able to give some time and thought to the cause.

You don't try to start big! Select some one or two objectives which would probably be of unquestioned value to all your prospective members if it existed. One logical choice for a starter would be the issuance of a directory or buyers' guide, a roster listing all those within the industry (or its division) for distribution to procurement personnel (also to sales managers). (See the next chapter on Directories for contents and the mechanics of publishing a directory or buyers' guide.)

For a very special, devious reason, it is suggested that another objective could be announced as a common mailing list. This envisions a compilation of customers in the territory, the names contributed by the prospective members, to be available to all under a predetermined set of rules and regulations. I am well aware that the problems of getting such a list together and in usable form are tremendous, almost insurmountable. You will no sooner mention it than there will be those who refuse to consider throwing their lists into the pot because they think *they* have names no one else has. (These people don't realize there are no secrets of that kind in a well covered territory! Even if there were, wouldn't *they*, in turn, receive the benefit of the other fellow's "secrets"?)

I said I was suggesting the common mailing list for a "special, devious reason": that is, you can be sure it takes a strongly established, clear thinking group to actually get such a list going — probably too difficult for an embryo association. BUT — just by bringing up such a controversial subject, you draw the sharp attention and aroused interest of prospective members to your proposed plans. As the debate ensues, one will be bound to say, "Instead of that, why don't we do thus-and-so?" giving his reasons. Others will agree. First thing you know, you will have an association *started* by virtue of the "thus-and-so" projects that begin to accumulate!

P.S. As to the "common mailing list" — you will find, if your group is of any size at all, that *some* of your compatriots will see the value of such a list and will be willing to poll their individual lists. And from that acorn, an oak will grow!   □

XXI

THE TRADE DIRECTORY/BUYERS' GUIDE

The why of it — and how to produce it

The benefits of a trade association publishing a directory of its membership are absolutely incalculable! With the possible exception of group insurance, there can be no better reason for the very existence of a trade association. Again and again, instances arise of how valuable such a compiled listing can be to those who participate. If your association provides a reasonably comprehensive publication, you will earn the gratitude of the trade. You relieve customers of the time-consuming irritations encountered wrestling with thick, clumsy phone books in trying to find names and phone numbers, hunting for elusive notations, searching files, trying to remember the whereabouts of calling cards that have a way of getting misplaced or lost. The trade will bless you for providing enough data to make it a serviceable buyers' guide, a thumbnail compilation of basic information needed by not only purchasing personnel *but also by sales managers*! I could all but fill another book with stories of how individual firms gained directly and indirectly from being listed in their association's directories, but one actual instance, told to me recently by the rep involved, will illustrate the point:

In the Northern California Chapter ERA's directory edited and published by the writer, pictures of the men heading up rep firms were being looked over by a New York manufacturer. One rep's picture in particular caught his attention. He recognized it as that of a man who had been a personal friend of his in the past but with whom he had lost touch some ten years before, after the friend moved to California. He reached for the phone and just caught the rep about to leave the office.

The greetings over, they delightedly exchanged amenities and chuckled over "remember when —?" reminiscences. Finally, the manufacturer spoke of his products, at the same time asking if his line might fit in with this rep's activities. As it happened, the rep was wide open to just such a class of line. They closed negotiations quickly. Then wot hoppen? In the first year, the rep did over a million dollars worth of business on that line!

Not always that dramatic but, in one way or another, I have heard many anecdotes about reps acquiring lines solely as a result of being listed in their directories, a very real plus aside from the primary purpose of being helpful to the customers.

The kind of directory to publish can vary from the simplicity of an inexpensive file folder or can even be made of ordinary stationery sheets, on out to the opulent printing of a many-page publication. What data or material to include in addition to members' names, addresses and phone numbers depends on how much money you are willing to spend. And, of course, who does the job governs its attractiveness, its usefulness and, above all, its accuracy.

In addition to the basic information supplied, you can take it a step or two further. You can show a breakdown of each rep members' activities by describing the territory he covers, listing employees by name, indicating what stocks are available locally from his warehouse or from distributors, or that orders are shipped only direct from the factory, that he specializes in distributor or industrial business as the case might be, displaying pictures of himself, his key men or office scenes.

At this point, even if your directory has no more data than

the foregoing, it already assumes value beyond what it means to the territory's purchasing personnel because of its special interest to *the sales manager* seeking representation in your territory. Some reps consider this advantage even more important than looking upon the publication as a "buyers' guide," reasoning that buyers don't mean anything if you don't have the lines to sell them!*

The directory becomes proportionately more valuable to the user if your members list the lines they carry by factory name and, even more desirable, follow each brand name with brief product descriptions. Still another extremely important compilation is a "manufacturers' index" section. That is, you list each manufacturer represented in your area first, followed by the name of the local rep and his phone number. In addition you might want to include a classified product section, showing under each grouped category those members who handle the product lines named.

Then, continuing to make your directory more elaborate, you might include a map showing the territory your association covers, a list of warranty stations perhaps, a general article explaining the activities of your association members, pictures of events in snapshots from conventions or from your local doings, maybe a recap of your past year's activities, a page showing pictures of your officers, your members classified according to trade activities if there are distinct categories in your industry and other inclusions that might be of interest to your particular trade.

I am quite aware that in many associations, the lack of a

---

* The over-enthusiasm on this point stems, however, from actual experience. In Northern California, our electronic directory is requested by many sales managers each year. Why would a sales manager be asking for a rep directory if he weren't seeking representation in the referenced territory?

membership directory is not so much questioning its value as is the problem of, first, how much the job is going to cost but, secondly, or perhaps the main consideration, who is to do it. Due to the average man's unfamiliarity with publishing, the magnitude of the job becomes exaggerated and the project often languishes, to be abandoned in wishful, empty thinking.

I'll grant you there has to be *somebody* in your group willing to be the spearhead in putting the project together for consideration, if not actually getting it under way. If you have only some twenty-five to fifty members in your association (or chapter) one or two volunteers ought to be able to handle the job. If some fifty to a hundred or more, it will take a committee of three people to do it. (I am visualizing something more than just issuing a list of members, addresses and phone numbers, although even that is better than nothing. You at least are rendering a bit of real service to your trade in providing them with such a list. If your organization can't do that much I would question why it exists at all!)

If your association has spirit, and grasps how valuable the promotion of such cooperative ventures can be to each participating member, it should not be too difficult to draw on your group for volunteers. It is preferable, if possible, to select men who have had some experience with printing beyond only buying stationery. Those who have compiled catalogs are your best bet. A good choice, too, would be from among reps who engage in frequent mailings of printed matter, who would have more than usual experience in dealing with printers.

Of course, ordinarily your best results would be turning the job over to professionals, such as advertising and public relations firms or perhaps others who might be making a specialized business of such work. Naturally, that will cost money! It might be well, however, before getting too scared, to obtain *several* preliminary quotations. They will vary tremendously! When you have these figures before you, pro-rating among the members might show the cost to be not at all prohibitive.

If your group has never had such a publication and there are enough of you enthused about it to give it serious consideration, I would suggest a procedure on this order:

Don't be too ambitious with your first edition: it isn't *necessary* to have a professional outfit take over your first job, even if your members *are* willing to spend the money! Start with volunteers! They are experienced in your industry! *They* know what the directory should incorporate. They know *what* should be featured as most important. They know what *the buyer* is most anxious to know. In other words, even though the first effort will not be too beautiful a printing job, it should be practical, down to earth in supplying the required information. With the first edition, the format or the printing of it aren't the most important matters — it's the *information* the publication supplies and *that* is best brought out by men who are in the business — your own members.

Then! with the publication of your first directory, you will have received an education! All through the year, you will have been gathering comments from the trade, learning what they like or what they don't care about in the directory, of what you omitted that should have been in there and what you can well do without.

By the time you are through with that first edition and ready for the second, your committee who got it out will have become "Semi-pros!" in knowing what the next one should be like. *They* can tell the professionals what is wanted in a way that could not have been done before the first go-around. And, you will find, with each successive edition, new ideas will keep cropping up, calculated to constantly improve the project.

And *this* is perhaps about as interesting and important for you to keep in mind as anything about issuing a directory; as the trade becomes more and more dependent on it, any of your members who were reluctant in the beginning about coming in, will find they *have* to be in! They will have become pretty tired of being forced to continue explaining to the customers *and to their principals* why they were omitted!

In the writer's home area, the far-reaching effectiveness of our Northern California Chapter Electronic Representative Association directory has been proved beyond question. While we devote a full page to each member's operation in detail and include features which turn the publication into a real trade guide in addition to its directory listings, as I said and suggested before, it is not necessary to undertake so elaborate a publication with one's first edition. However, as of possible interest and guidance, an example of the form we use for compiling the member's data and how to fill it out is reproduced at the end of this chapter.

Note that this form is set up in triplicate. After the member fills it out, the original goes to the typographer who sets the type, the second copy is kept by the editor for his reference as the job progresses and the third copy is kept by the member for his files. Incidentally, one secret of the reputation our directory has for dependability is the thorough-going proofings we give it. If your directory isn't practically 100% accurate, its effectiveness takes a tremendous drop.

Assuming that in your first edition it may be too much to undertake including a full page for each member, the information called for can be set out grouped three or four members to a page — or you can compress the data into closely printed paragraphs, each member's data to follow in single column line. In that way, employing two columns, you can run even twenty sets of data to a page and still have the information readable, which makes for a very economical job.

Well, gents — you can do as you may please about issuing a directory to your trade but, if for no other reason, isn't this a graphic, honest example of that very real *service* reps are always so fond of bragging about? And that brings up another facet of publishing a directory: there are some associations who accept and solicit advertising for its pages, by way of defraying cost of the publication, even perhaps to the extent of showing a tidy profit. In some cases, that is entirely fitting — running ads paid for by your principals, perhaps getting local hotels to advertise because you have so many out-of-town visitors who might be enticed into putting up with them, ditto for restaurants and so on.

The objections are that (a) this "commercializing" the directory detracts from the aura of *giving* the customer something of value at your cost and (b) the people advertising begin to have something to say for their money and it may become necessary to bend in their direction, thereby losing sight of the publication's aim. However, it could be the pragmatic course to take if the project's costs otherwise seem to be too much of an obstacle.

The association member pays his pre-determined share of the directory's cost, assuming your officers or delegated committee has met, discussed and explored the project, readied it for presentation to the membership with determination of its cost. The discussion has been made that participation of each member either be optional or that an assessment be made mandatory on each member if the latter ruling has been found to be legal. (Check this with your attorney.) The project has been put to a vote, accepted, and the word is "Go." Now, one very important point: establish a firm rule at the very beginning, to the effect that the member must attach his check to the data he sends in for inclusion in the directory. Don't put his obligation on the basis of *billing* him, for payment at some later time — 'tain't advisable! If you don't collect *before* the directory is printed, regardless of how well intentioned your membership may be, you'll be wading up to your navel in collection problems for months to come!

Point up that none of you are bill collectors, that the member can't expect the association to finance him, that if he wants in, *his check and his data* must be received by such-and-such a deadline — and make it plain that you *do* mean *deadline*! You might offer only this one concession; make postdated checks acceptable. Since it will be two or three months from the time the project starts until finished and the bills for payment come in, you might fix a time like sixty days for a check to be postdated. But insist nevertheless that such a check accompany a member's data.

Observance of the foregoing will forestall untold grief afterwards because of delinquent members.

Use your judgment as to how much time the member is given before reaching the deadline but don't give him *too* much time because the longer you are willing to wait for his data, the more time he will take. Not only is it human to procrastinate but the continual changes in this business keep the rep in a constant state of flux. If you wait for the last word, you'll never go to print. You just have to arbitrarily set your deadlines and stay with your decision.

On costs: it is well to have at least three respected printers bid on the job. Printing! In no other industry have I encountered such variations in pricing. I have had quotations on major jobs like this differ as much as hundreds of percent — from supposedly sizable, long established printing houses. So, shop!

By this time, I am sure you have come to the realization that the one or more in charge of the project had better be pretty strong minded, firmly determined not to make exceptions or relax the rules unless a member has some extremely valid reason for such an action. You have got to place authority in the hands of whoever is handling the project and be prepared with full backup if some one individual persists in calling for things to be done in some exceptional way more to his purpose or liking.

The point is this: it is not necessary to be a dictator but we have to remember the same old story, that reps are individualists. If you ask ten reps for their opinions on a subject, you'll get that many opinions. Each one will have his own ideas about the matter. So it is with your directory: though a rep hasn't had any more printing experience than ordering letterheads for his firm, he will nevertheless have *his* ideas of what a directory should be like. Again — in this case, one of the oldest but truest cliches of all — you can't please everybody.

So — get all your ideas and wishes into the basket in the beginning, when the project is just a-borning. Take your consensus. Lay down the rules accordingly and stick to them! That's *the* only way you'll be able to come out with a good job, and within a reasonable period of time. And the one member (there's bound to be one!) who grumbles because it wasn't done his way, will nevertheless benefit from the results in the long run, just like everybody else.

EXAMPLE OF A FORM TO BE FILLED OUT BY MEMBERS FOR INCLUSION
IN A TRADE ASSOCIATION DIRECTORY (OR BUYERS' GUIDE)

Here insert picture and name of "head man"	*REP COMPANY NAME IN THIS SPACE* *(Use same size and type style for all members)* *Street address_____* *City and ZIP_____* *Phone number here* *(include area code) TWX here*	*If second picture (as of partner or manager) subject's picture and name goes here*

PERSONNEL

    Office   *Outside*

List individual names of owner and employees here. (If member does not wish names to be separated under the two sub-headings, cross out the words "office" and "outside")

LINES REPRESENTED

Here list all principals' names - in alphabetical order, followed by brief descriptions of their products.

Use capital letters or underline the manufacturer's formal name, to distinguish it from the product descriptions.... Admonish members to TYPE all data.

For uniformity and best appearance, hold each product line to one line of printing... Space each typed line well away from the one that follows, so that the printer can easily read the copy.

If the member wishes to show he is stocking or warehousing one or more product lines, have him place an asterisk* before the principal's name. Along with this, instruct the printer to insert at the bottom of the member's page:
* STOCKED LOCALLY.

If members specialize in trade categories, this could be shown on the member's page - for example:

Distributor____ Industrial_____ Consumer Products____

Warranty service____ etc., etc.

At bottom of the page, wind up with:
ABOVE INFORMATION SUPPLIED AND AUTHORIZED BY:

Company name_____Signature_____ Date

XXII

QUIRKS ARE THE RULE –
AS WELL AS THE EXCEPTION

Every rep his own psychologist

A statesman is one who explains to his wife that the reason he didn't come home until the late hour of 3 a.m. was because he had to attend a prolonged committee meeting. A politician is one who makes her believe it.

Successful selling is largely dependent upon the extent to which one has observed and come to know characteristics of human behavior, of how individuals may be expected to react in a given set of circumstances. This is not to take a pretentious stand, of inferring that any person in this world has accumulated enough wisdom for definitive conclusions about the human mind. Of course not! The point is, however, that experience with the Homo sapiens under a given set of circumstances, combined with knowing one's business, enables reasonably applicable judgments to be formed upon which the sales person can act.

Upon opening a new store in a shopping center, a haberdasher decided to try a mailer by way of promoting "get acquainted" business. He drew up the copy, centering upon an exceptionally fine men's shirt at an extremely low price as a "come in" inducement. He got surprisingly little response. Undiscouraged, but recognizing his own limitations, he

turned to a well recommended advertising specialist to re-
vamp the mailer copy, being still unable to understand why
that genuine bargain hadn't drawn the customers. The pro's
changes didn't seem to be very dramatic — just some slight
alterations in format, a few phrases re-worded here and there,
but one difference drew a mild protest from the merchant.
The copy again featured the shirt but included the wording,
"Sizes in stock: 14, 15, 15½, 16, 16½ and 17. Sleeve lengths
from 32 to 35."

"Why use up good space with that?" the merchant asked.
"Everyone knows the sizes of men's shirts."

"People have learned to be skeptical, even cynical about
advertising," replied the other. "Noting how extremely low
you've priced the shirt, they assume you have only a few
scattered numbers in stock, being used simply as bait, that
when they come in, you'll try to sell them something else.
But when you spell it out like this, you're laying it right on
the line — they know you mean it."

When *that* mailer went out, the stock of those shirts sold
out in a few days. The large number of customers it brought
in made it necessary for the merchant to hire an additional
clerk.

*   *   *

The gap between the average person in sales and the
professional may not appear to be wide, but it is there. Take
a situation like this: the average salesman, for instance, making friendly conversation with a prospective customer, will
speak of how much mileage he gets out of his car, of how he
controls the weed growth in his garden, of how difficult it is
for him to buy shoes that fit, of the places he intends to visit
on his next vacation — and so on and on. But the *professional*
salesman, likewise making friendly conversation with a prospective customer, would ask *him* how much mileage *he* gets
out of *his* car, enquires how *he* controls the weeds in *his*
garden, questions whether or not *he* has difficulty buying

shoes that fit *him*, and what *his* choice is for his next vacation — and so on — ultimately to walk out with the order in his pocket, leaving behind a customer thinking to himself, "Now there's a good salesman. He doesn't waste a person's time with idle chit-chat — he gets on with it. Real friendly, too — I like that kind — no high pressure — wish there were more around like him, people who don't just talk, talk about themselves" . . .

Quoting that hypothetical customer could have come word for word from real life. There's nothing unusual about people being engrossed in themselves — every one of us! We seldom realize how much of what we say is based upon ourselves. But that is what goes to making the rep a *professional* — when he knows the rewards of being a good listener, of encouraging people to talk about themselves, by restraining his own natural desire to talk about himself, saving his ego for his homecoming, for the one who promised to love, share and listen to him for ever and ever plus a day.

*   *   *

The wanderer

One of the common and most frustrating situations confronting the salesman is the prospect whose attention has wandered away from the sales talk. His eyes are fixed narrowly, as though in deep, attentive thought, but his mind is on his golf game, or is occupied with surveying the full figured cutie standing at the desk across the room, or wondering whether or not he's going to get that raise he asked for and a variety of unrelated thoughts far removed from the salesman's attempts to make an impression. I know one rep who, faced with this problem, has a trick of lapsing into a string of double-talk, meaningless gibberish, suddenly hitting the desk with the flat of his hand as though to emphasize a point — which abruptly brings the prospect back to the immediate scene. Whereupon the rep asks, "Isn't that right?," watching the other struggle to recall what had just been said.

No doubt this is effective and probably amusing but, as a pro would realize, you don't make friends by making your customer uncomfortable, even for a moment.

A smoother, more productive and harmless little trick for getting the prospect's wandering attention back to the subject in hand is to break off a sentence in mid-air. In the sudden, ensuing silence, you reach for a pen and quite ostentatiously set the point down in a piece of paper, as though about to start writing. The dreamer's faraway thoughts are interrupted by the abruptly unexpected silence and the movement before him; his eyes are drawn to the pen, his mind now expecting something about to be written — and he's back, listening to what the *professional* has to say.

*   *   *

Let my sample go, dummy!

From the reception room where I was seated, awaiting my turn to be interviewed, I could see through the glass partition and idly watched the salesman who had entered the buyer's office just ahead of me. He was manipulating a sample of what seemed to be a slide switch, uniquely activated by pushing a lever rather than the conventional sliding push-button principle. Hunched over the device, he fascinatedly worked the lever while the mechanism reacted accordingly. He was evidently deeply intrigued by the apparent ingenuity of the thing. I could not hear him, of course, but from under his lowered head I guessed he was mumbling rather than talking directly to the buyer who, in the meantime, was interestedly following the movements of the switch with his eyes, even twisting his head for a better view.

I was almost beside myself. "Why the hell doesn't he hand the sample to the buyer, the damned fool! Look at how the man is trying to get

a look at it!" As though I had spoken aloud, the
buyer reached across the desk and took the sample
out of the salesman's hands.

It's mighty poor salesmanship, indeed amateurish, if one fails to realize the importance of allowing the prospect to handle the product himself. Many an article will help sell itself if you can just get it into the buyer's close range. The selling of automobiles is a commonplace example; we all know one of the first things the auto salesman tries is to get you into the car and have you drive it yourself. If it's good enough for the automotive industry — ! —

What happens when you buy a necktie? You look down into the showcase and point to one that interests you. The clerk brings it out, forms it expertly into a knot around his finger and holds it up for you to judge the effect. What do you do? You reach across, take the tie into your own hands, to fumble awkwardly while you try, as the clerk did, to make it appear knotted. You want to examine it closely, handle it yourself — despite the fact that you're selecting a tie for how it impresses others when you are wearing it, not what it looks like to you at close range.

The moral is: if it's smaller than a bread box, get it into his hands. If bigger — well — whenever practical, the sooner you establish contact intimacy between the buyer and your product, the more likely he is to buy it.

*   *   *

Turn over in your mind what bothers *you* when *you* are the prospective customer. Now, reverse the roles: are you *sure* you refrain from committing the very same disturbing acts that bother you when *you* are buying? Just because the surrounding circumstances are somewhat different, you may be perpetrating the very same disagreeable actions that you criticize in those who wait on you. No? Are you sure? It happens *very* commonly. How about this one?

In the case of a customer you see repeatedly, do you reach out, grasp his hand and shake it vigorously every time you call? Many do — not realizing that the customer is fully aware all this great show of brotherly love is because you are after his business. Isn't it entirely possible the customer may not care to feel the salesman's sweaty palm and wishes the man would get on with whatever he is there for? Unless you haven't seen your man for a long time and there might be indeed a pleasurable moment in renewing contact, or in the case of, perhaps, introducing yourself to a new prospect, there *might* be some reason for the handshaking business but, otherwise, you'd do well to wait until the other fellow makes the first move.

*   *   *

Few problems confront the businessman where human nature looms up so important as in the hiring of a salesman for your staff. To fully cover *that* subject is far beyond the scope of this work but I'm going to take up enough space to point up a particularly revealing attitude in a prospective employee which isn't always given the importance it deserves by the person doing the interviewing. It has to do with the applicant's previous occupation. As a f'r instance:

Let's suppose the applicant were to say, "Yeah, I was in the insurance business but that's a lousy business — that's why I got out." Now, no standard business deserves the term "lousy" or an equivalent thereof. When thousands and thousands of people have been and still are engaged in a well-known, long-established, legitimate occupation, such sweeping condemnations tell you much about the speaker. It's a good bet that this fellow is always going to be finding fault with something or somebody other than himself.

Suppose he had said, "Insurance is all right but not for me. It's too slow for my temperament. I like more action — " or something of that kind, with the emphasis on why he prefers *your* kind of business, rather than on drastically knocking another occupation. That would be a *good* sign.

*   *   *

A rep particularly liked by the trade (and this explains one reason why) has made a practice of giving special attention to any buyer on whom he has been calling who has undergone an important change of position — to a new department with perhaps more importance than he had previously, or to another company or some change of a substantial nature in the buyer's life. This rep takes the time and trouble to write the man a little note, congratulating him, if that seems to be called for, or just generally wishing him well in his new position.... Give it a try! and watch how extra-cordial welcome you will be next time you call on that man! He won't forget you!

*   *   *

This one-man new rep operation, unable to afford a secretary and to finance advertising himself, went at it like this:

He keeps a mailing list of customers and prospects conveniently at hand on his desk, along with a supply of mailers, envelope "stuffers" etc. and a stack of envelopes. Each evening, when he comes back to the office after a day's calls, he takes a couple of minutes to stuff and address a handful of envelopes, and drops them into a mailbox on his way home. He spends only a few moments at the end of the day on it — no sweat, no big deal, the stationery and postage costs minor, and so he gets out quite respectable size mailings rather painlessly, so to speak.

*   *   *

A tip: nothing new about this, but so many reps still use rubber stamping on catalogs, so easily smeared or otherwise hard to decipher, instead of the self-adhesive labels now so inexpensive — especially appropriate on hard-coated stock catalog covers — besides adding a note of distinction.

*   *   *

A very hard-working rep friend of mine, now long retired, was one of those who always tried to get in "just one more call" before winding up his working day. As a result, he seldom returned to the office before his secretary left for the day. It was his practice to carry a supply of 3 x 5 cards loose in his coat pocket. Whenever a call developed some chore which ultimately the girl would be taking care of — a catalog request, an invoice error to be corrected, to send a customer a price sheet, and the like — he would note what was to be done on a card, along with the applicable names.

Back at the office, he would simply dump the cards out on the girl's desk, ready for her to start working on as soon as she arrived in the morning. No need for him to stand around, taking up the time of both while he gave her the individual instructions. The card notes told her what to do, and he was soon on his way, to take care of more critical matters.

*   *   *

> *Any man who, for any reason whatsoever, fails to make absolutely sure that his phone is answered properly, would do better to find himself some occupation other than that of manufacturers' representation. Damage very often beyond repair, and the reason unknown to the employer, can be done by phone calls being poorly answered. There is no need of estimating how dependent the rep business is on the phone; you can depend on the fact that its very existence is!*

That girl who answers the phone in a dull, insipid, couldn't-care-less voice, reflects *you*, the owner of the business . . . The one who answers the phone in a snappy, "Yes, yes — you're interrupting me — what do you want?" kind of manner is even worse when it comes to giving a caller a poor opinion of your firm . . . But let's take a look at a few examples which are fairly common, so much so that apparently the employer isn't aware of them because (at least, so one would think!) he would take steps to correct them:

The phone rings, the secretary answers, and this follows:
Caller: "I'd like to speak to Mr. Soandso — is he there?"
Secretary: Instead of answering his questions, *she* asks one: "Who's calling?"

After the caller has identified himself, she may have to tell him Mr. Soandso is out. The caller wonders — is the guy *really* out? Is he ducking me? Am I too unimportant for him to talk to me? Who the hell does he think he is? . . . It would be so much better for the secretary to say, "I'll see if he's in, sir — may I have your name, please?" So that, if the caller really is a pest whom you want to duck but without giving offense, there are more tactful ways to do it.

Another no-no: the caller has waited patiently for Mr. Soandso, until finally the secretary responds with, "Yes, sir, he's in — I'll let you talk to him now."

"Let?" The caller who knows his English thinks to himself, "Is she that important, that I need *her* permission to talk to her boss?"
MORAL: there may be a number of reasons why you're not getting orders from a prospect, all of which can perhaps be overcome — but of one thing you can be sure: hurt his ego and you're dead.

How about this one? The phone rings and is answered:
Secretary: Good morning — the Repboss Company, Jenny Cheery speaking — may I help you?
(Fine, gives the caller a nice, welcome feeling.)
Caller: I'd like to talk with Joe Repboss.
Secretary: Sorry, he isn't in.
(Silence. The caller waits for more. Nothing. No more. The temperature starts dropping.)
Caller: Well - *will* he be in today?
Secretary: Oh, yes.

(And again she goes dumb.)
Caller, (his ire rising inversely as the temperature drops):
When *will* he be in? This morning? Tomorrow? Next year?
(Finally, she tells him when the boss will be in — or at least
hazards a guess — but the caller's first favorable impression
has been dispelled.)

Some secretaries — well meaning, but overdoing it — try
too hard to conserve their employer's time by handling a call
themselves. She should, indeed, ask if she can be of help in
the boss' absence, but to refrain from being persistent. It can
easily be carried to the point of irritation. On this score
especially, a good move is to have some friend of yours call
and see how she docs on this point. If she needs correction,
whatever you do, don't discourage her desire to try and be
helpful to the caller, but to analyze the procedure for her so
that she gets the idea and can then carry out this touchy little
situation properly.

A prominent rep of my acquaintance, operating a quite
sizable enterprise, has a man answering the office phone
rather than a girl. I suppose the lady libbers will cry male
chauvinism at his reasoning (t'ain't me, Ms!) but the thinking
is that the customer prefers the authoritative sounding voice
of a man, to whom he can presumably immediately explain
his requirements — as opposed to having to go through an
intermediary, namely a girl, who herself wouldn't be expected to have the answers. I suppose this depends largely on
the nature of the business. I would assume, as in this case,
such a practice might be more acceptable in a technical rather
than the everyday kind of business. But — it's something to
think about especially if, as the trend now goes, one tries to
do business over the phone in substitution for calls in person.

Incidentally, this might be a good place to interpose the
situation of an unthinking rep I used to know who became

highly indignant when called to the phone to take a request for a catalog or to quote some price from a standard list. He would storm about the office whenever his great, ponderous stream of consciousness was interrupted by his secretary telling him she had a call for him if, upon taking up the phone, the call turned out to be a simple matter which she could easily have handled herself.

What couldn't get through into this guy's thick skull was the fact that he had spent many years building himself up to the trade, establishing his identification, his "popularity" if you will. That customers as a matter of fact asked for him by name was a tribute to his own efforts, though he failed to recognize it as such. If he felt his time in the office was too valuable to be bothered answering the phone, wouldn't it be simple for his secretary to be instructed to tell the caller, tentatively, that she "just wasn't sure" if the man being called for was available — was there something *she* might be able to help out on? From the reaction, wouldn't it be easy to determine whether or not she ought to pass the call on?

On the other hand: if the caller was asking for a catalog or a price, might that not be actually a fortuitous time for the rep to follow up quickly, to pitch, since it was evident that the caller was interested in something this rep had for sale? □

XXII

RETIREMENT HAS ITS DRAWBACKS

Eldorado may not be all you expected—unless —

I suppose you must have heard, in one form or another, about men being unable to stand retirement, who up and died after quitting their life work. These stories always bring on warnings about the need for keeping busy in order to stay alive and well. Right? Yes, old hat, admittedly. But what THEY don't tell you is why retired *manufacturers' representatives* in particular, despite observance of such well meant admonitions, can become disenchanted with the retired life, even sometimes wishing they had continued in business for at least "just a few years longer." It is a strange state of mind, difficult to understand in view of the fact that you no longer have to contend with the misery of traffic-choked streets, with the mad rushing, the clock watching, the to-and-fro hopping about, the endless searching for customers, the sales managers who could never be satisfied, the temperamental secretaries always threatening to quit, the expediters who blame the rep for all their companies' woes, and all the rest of the battles. Yes, you've paid your dues — so why aren't you happy?

Could be one or more of several reasons. One might be in connection with your friends: having long looked forward to the fun, you assume you ought to be getting together with them often now that you've got the time — like attend a ballgame, talk politics, swap stories, maybe play a little poker. Except that — now — *they* don't have the time! Some are still too busy working in their own enterprises, or they've reached the age when they can talk only about their aches and pains, or they're already dead.

> *Voltaire said, "If God did not exist, it would be necessary to invent Him." The old iconoclast was a seer. God has been put away. MAN himself is now an idolatrous object of worship, with THEY for a church and what THEY SAY the bible. So, THEY SAY: when you've accumulated enough worldly goods so that you don't have to work any more, you are now expected to spend your time fishing, golfing, sailing or some version or other of sport pleasures. THEY SAY also that you may put in time digging in the garden, building model aeroplanes and other such pastimes. But before that, of course you must have travelled around the country or abroad, outside of your own parish, that is; the travelling syndrome being especially basic dogma no true believer in what THEY SAY dares to violate.*
>
> *Well, so, okay — you've been doing the fun routine — the much vaunted traveling, the popular sports, the visits with your adorable grandchildren, the inconsequential hobbies — but for how long can you continue leading this life that gives you no* sense *of* ACHIEVEMENT — and THAT is what your retired rep's discontent is all about! *It lies in the temperament, the philosophy and the character of the kind of man drawn to the rep business. He is by nature a planner and a doer, an administrator, a leader, an innovator. This isn't a man who has to be admonished to keep busy! Hell's fire — to be on the go is this man's natural, normal state. But — now he's bored!*

The trouble lies in the fact that he was fooled. He was misled into believing the aim of existence was to bring about that Nirvana THEY consider beautiful but, to *him*, is a life of idleness, a contradiction of his true nature. This man has spent all his adult years in the chase, the ever-striving battle to make the buck, now brought to a cease-fire stop. It's like being geared up to driving for so many years on the turnpikes and freeways at speeds of 60 to 90 miles an hour, suddenly to be slowed down to crawling along in low gear. Okay, Mr. Reader — you scoff! Today, that is! I know — you say, lead me to it — that's the life for me! But ah, my friend — *you're going to learn!*

No, it won't happen right away — but, eventually, retired, in time the day will come when you ask yourself, "Well, wonder what I can do today." And you continue "wondering" as you yawn and dawdle over still another cup of coffee and pore through parts of the newspaper you ordinarily wouldn't find any use for other than the floor of the parakeet's cage. You don't feel like gathering your gear together to go out, and you grimace at the prospect of another tedious day of hanging around the house, seeking out or manufacturing things to do — "to keep busy." You looked at the reflection in the bathroom mirror that morning and scowled — you didn't even think it worth the effort to shave that aging puss. No, you just can't put your finger on it but something is wrong — very wrong. This business of being retired hasn't been proving up to what it was cracked up to be. And if it keeps dragging along like this, you're liable to crack up yourself.

Well, what is the answer, then? Is it never to retire? Or, having once quit, go back to work as of the old days? Back to grinding away on the highways, catering to smart buyers a generation younger than yours, trying to learn all over again the changes in products, in prices and trade personnel that transpired since you left the field?

Ridiculous! Of course not!

There *is* an answer and, to this writer, insofar as manufacturers' representatives are concerned, I firmly believe it is *the* answer. Namely: it lies in EGO! the consciousness of self, that something within a man which impels him to be Somebody without which, conversely, he's nobody. And, it's what retirement can do to a man's ego that breaks up the retired rep's euphoria.

When the rep was in business, life moved like a continuous universal machine — of which he was a part. He served a purpose, was needed, useful. Today — retired — the machine roars on without him; he isn't even missed! And *that* is hard on a man who, if he was a rep by temperament, by choice as well as occupation, *had* to be a man with well developed ego. If that man attained sufficient affluence as a manufacturers' representative to retire, it follows that he was possessed of *that driving need for self-fulfillment* without which he would never have achieved the success that enabled him to retire!

That man won't get the satisfaction out of living the retired life if it's going to mean piddling all his time away on the golfing and fishing order. Like desserts at the dinner table, sports are treats — for weekends, for occasional holiday outings — but the real bread-and-butter of life has always come out of working week-days. Here again, one may quote that, "Plus ca change, plus c'est la meme chose" and if I remember enough of my few weeks of high school French, that breaks down into, "Things just don't change." Which includes people. In short: no matter what — if he's still breathing, that erstwhile rep's drive instinct is still there and consequently that man needs challenge, competition and the rewards of reaching a difficult goal in order to be happy.

How fortunate, indeed, is the ex-rep who foresightedly prepared his SOMETHING CONSTRUCTIVE TO DO with all that wonderful, glorious, *free* time now on his hands. Like, what? Oh, good Lord — so many possibilities! One man anticipates a desire to keep on "selling" — to him it's fun, providing he can name his own time and place. He might have taken up night courses while still in business — studying, perhaps, the intricacies of real estate or insurance, maybe languages in preparation for doing some importing-exporting. Another would perhaps write special articles for trade publications by way of becoming known as an industry authority, after retirement to go in for consulting — and so on and on.

It would be pointless for this writer to specify any particular career for the retired rep to follow any more than to recommend his own because each of us has his own tastes, talents and desires, with innumerable variations in family needs, in personal circumstances, in environment, in physical condition — it's up to each one to go *his* way — but, GO! Plan in advance — now! — for that *second* career! Even though financial need becomes a thing of the past, the important thing is to keep on going — at your own elected pace, at whatever it may be but an occupation of the kind that keeps the adrenalin moving, SOMETHING which, to an erstwhile rep, will be considered ACHIEVEMENT because *that* is what it takes to keep a real rep happy!   □

Anecdotage and Curiosa

CONTENTS

FROM STICK TO TREE IN TWO MOVES

Of course I enjoy the sight of flowers and shrubbery around our house but, myself, I'm not much of a gardener. That's the distaff's department. In consequence, it forestalls much discussion when my wife resorts to hiring a neighbor's teen-age boy to help out with the weeding and such. She says, philosophically, it helps kids build character — with which I hasten to agree.

She came home one day with some new plants, to show me a special bonus she had received from the nursery she patronizes. I looked questioningly at her prize.

"It's a cherry tree," she announced stoutly.

I took it in my hand — a stick about a half-inch thick by some eighteen inches long. No branches. No roots. No nuthin' — just a stick.

"This is a tree?"

"Well, naturally, it has to be planted and then it will grow."

Amused by her faith in this piece of wood, and our current assistant gardener being away just then at Boy Scouts Camp, I magnanimously offered to plant it for her. "Where do you want it?" I asked. "A cherry tree will look very nice in front of the house," she replied.

She selected a spot that seemed suitable, where it would get the morning sun. I dug a hole, shoved the stick down into it, and patted the soil back in place. Prompted by the fact that I had done all this work by myself, I felt I had a vested interest in the project now and kept watch, waiting to see my efforts bloom into a fine big tree loaded down with luscious cherries. I hoped they would be the deep red kind. I remembered my mother used to make a wonderfully delicious jam of cherries; the very thought made my mouth water.

But nothing happened. Not that year. Nor the next. Not one single sign of life. For some two years, it stayed there, unchanged in any way, just as I had planted it — a stick stuck into the ground. M'Lady decided to put in a row of flowers in that area, so I yanked the silly thing up, to get it out of her way. I was going to toss it into our fireplace but it didn't seem dry enough to burn readily.

What prompted me, I don't know. I had become accustomed to watching that stick and, I guess, had sort of become attached to it. Maybe I thought I needed the exercise. Anyway — I found a bare spot, this time in back of the house, where it would be bathed in the afternoon sun. I dug a hole and re-planted it there.

What followed was like magic. Within months, that stick sprouted tiny greenish bumps, which developed into branches from which came full blown leaves. By the second year, it was several feet tall. The third year, it really took off and, to our delight, one Spring saw it covered with blossoms. In the following year, we really did become excited — you'd have thought we were having an addition to the family when we spotted one lone but unmistakably bright red cherry tucked away among the leaves! I got my camera out and took a picture of it — just before the birds got it.

At this writing, that change in location has produced for us a lovely, ten-foot tree. It blossoms beautifully in the Spring, growing a sizable quantity of cherries. (Nope — no jam — the birds get 'em!) We are so pleased with it; we don't even touch the sucker growth pushing up around its base, forming what we speak of as "our cherry orchard."

The incident set me to wondering about the many men who lead humdrum, unproductive, stunted lives. How might they fare if transferred to entirely new locations? How many are there "born to blush unseen," their talents unplumbed, dormant, for whom a transplanting in environment might bring out latent potentialities? What would be the influence of new occupations, new people, new surroundings? Would such a migration be disastrous or would a great flowering take place? Would the results be a transformation from Dullsville into the glory of achievement?

I suppose only Fate would have the answers, but isn't it a thought with which to conjure? Along with the fact that HOPELESS is only a WORD — not a fact? □

STORY OF AN (IN)FAMOUS GATE-CRASHER

Every business has its credit problems

Remember the chapter about the need for instant credit information? That problem isn't exclusive to repping, and thereby hangs an unusual story. It was told to me some years ago by one of the shrewdest businessmen I was ever fortunate enough to meet. Aside from his business acumen, Al H——— was a man of whose whimsy it was said that he couldn't announce he was going to lunch without pointing the fact up with an applicable anecdote.

During one of the two brief periods when I wasn't in business for myself, Mr. H——— employed me as a department manager in his radio business. Aside from the fact that he paid well, one satisfaction of being associated with Al was derived from those stories of his. He so loved to tell them, employing an odd knack of relating his tales as though reading from formal print. They were original, always entertaining, leading inevitably to an edifying point and, though occasionally a bit on the blue side, never really in bad taste. The one I am going to repeat here has to do with a rather delicate credit situation, an incident arising during the pursuit of what is sometimes termed, "the world's oldest profession."

We were putting on a highly advertised sale of the "ten dollars down, ten dollars a month" variety. It was going over big. Al walked into my department, somewhat separated from the parts sections, just as I had seated a customer buying one of the more expensive bargain radios. I was asking him the questions embodied in the store's lengthy credit application form. The man spotted Al and jumped up, calling out, "Why Mr. H————! Of all people! Long time no see. How've you been?"

Al responded with a hearty handshake and a big, toothy smile, returning the greeting with, "Well, well, well, you old rascal — and how are you?"

With this exchange of enquiries about their respective states of well being settled, the man turned to me and, pointing over his shoulder at Al said, "There you are — ask Mr. H———— who I am. He'll tell you I'm okay." He looked back questioningly at Al.

"Sure," Al responded loudly and, with a sweeping, somewhat grandiose gesture said, "He's okay. Uh — excuse me — I have to make an important phone call. Well — nice to see you again," and turned to walk away.

Nodding agreeably to the customer, I observed, "Indeed, yes — I can see you're old friends." I indicated the chair he had vacated at Al's entrance, the latter having disappeared after a final, friendly wave of his hand. "You said — " I referred to the credit form. "You've been working at this place for how long?"

He frowned. Before he could put into words the protest forming, I said, "It's not important — now — but I just have to fill in all these spaces or our bookkeeper — she's awfully old-maidish about these things — she'll give me hell. Just a formality. So if you don't mind — how long did you say?" Despite his grumpiness, I carried him completely through the entire form, question after question. Soon as the statement was checked, which wouldn't take long, I assured him, we'd deliver his purchase.

He had no more than left when Al, who must have been watching from a distance, strode back to my desk. He looked down at the credit form. I gathered his nod was of approval, but I felt I had to apologize. "Sorry to put your friend through all the routine, Al — force of habit, I guess. Besides, if you should ever want to cash your paper with a finance company, I'm sure you know they would insist — "

"Of course! You fill out the credit form!" he barked. "That's what I have them printed for! You take this guy — I meet lots of people — how the hell would I know if he's any good or not?"

He chuckled. "Young man — I have to explain something to you." His voice taking on a dramatic ring, he started:

Back in the years when I was about your age, we had a — uh — what do you call this fellow who they're always talking about, who gets into big sporting events without paying, who turns up at society parties where he wasn't invited?

O, sure — I know — you mean — I just can't think of his name — but the whole country knows him for his fame as a gate-crasher —

Exactly — that's the one. Well, in those years, we had a character who was famous throughout the West as a gate-crasher. However, his specialty was getting through — uh — well — h'mm — what we called sporting houses — if you know what I mean.

Yes, Al — I'm over twenty-one.

Well — this reputation as a non-paying patron was spreading from one — uh — house to another. One day, he got into a town new to him, made some enquiries and was directed to a well known — uh — that kind of house. There was no one in the lobby when he got there so he climbed the stairs and knocked at the first door he came to. The gal opened the door, took one look, let out an "Oh, No!" and started to close the door in his face. He braced his shoulder against the door and managed to keep it open.

"What's wrong?" he demanded. "Don't you work here?"

"What's wrong is I know who you are are! Someone pointed you out to me the last place I worked in — and I heard all about how you put it over on us poor workin' girls, so I'm tellin' you. You want service, you're goin' to have to pay in advance! Otherwise, nothin' doin', dearie, unless Madam okays you."

"You're out of your mind," he shrugged, "but I'll just have to show you — your Madam will okay me. Where do I find her?"

"Downstairs — first door to your right."

He descended and knocked at the designated door. The Madam, a portly, jewel-bedecked woman, opened the door and heartily greeted what was evidently a new customer to her. "Say," he said indignantly, "what's with your girl up there in that front room? She thinks I've got some kind of venereal disease and won't take me on. What kind of stupid — "

"Well — have you?"

"Of course not! Look for yourself."

He opened up his trousers. She examined the designated area closely, her experienced eye quickly making an expert diagnosis. She shook her head disgustedly. "It's so hard to get girls who know this business nowadays." She strode to the foot of the stairs and called out the girl's name, who came out of her room and looked down over the banister questioningly.

"This man is okay!" yelled the Madam. "You can take him on—it's all right." She turned back apologetically to the customer. "She's a new girl with me — I'm sorry." As he ascended the stairs, she called after him cheerily, "Have fun!"

"So," Al concluded, returning to his normal voice, "as far as I am concerned, they're all okay — but fill out the credit form!" □

A BUSINESS MAN BECOMES
A MALE CHAUVINIST

A mechanically minded school teacher had developed, as a result of his hobby, an intriguing new version of a commonly used tool — quite ingenious but, to market it, would require extended selling efforts for which he was unprepared with experience or the requisite finances.

Sensing the possibility of a profitable investment, a rep acquaintance offered to take over the entire marketing of the device in exchange for exclusive selling rights. The teacher enthusiastically agreed to a deal based tentatively on the showing of initial results in the rep's territory. The rep pitched in with an intensive campaign and the tool began to sell in goodly quantities.

His efforts created some demand, soon to be felt by others in the business. Whereupon he learned, to his dismay, that the product was now being obtained by several distributors directly from the "manufacturer," that he was being entirely bypassed on such business. Upon calling his "principal," the man's wife answered the phone, to inform him that her husband had to attend to his school duties, that she had taken over operation of the business.

When the rep brought up the matter of his agreement and his plaint that she was selling the product to others directly, without compensation to him, she became verbosely indignant. She couldn't see why he thought *he* "owned" the business, what right *he* had to tell *her* to whom she could sell, that "just *everybody*" was giving her orders and she certainly wasn't going to confine such a gold mine exclusively to one customer because the business wouldn't even have existed if *she* hadn't kept things going while her husband was fooling away his time in his shop, neglecting his school job, tinkering with things like this — until, unable to get a word in edgewise, the rep hung up.

Since he still hadn't recovered enough in commission or profit for his promotional efforts and, it being obvious that trying to work with this woman would only be a togethermess, he simply sold out the stock and dropped the whole thing.

A few months later, the lady appeared at his office, virtually demanding to know why he had stopped handling the product after claiming he was doing such big things with it, that other people were no longer giving her orders because they said it wasn't being promoted and that therefore they had no calls for the product and, in view of his promises to her husband, it proved he just wasn't a man of his word . . . .

The rep reached for his hat, pleaded an important appointment and fled . . . . That afternoon, he phoned his own wife to dress in her best, that he had tickets for the most talked about show in town, that they were going to have dinner at one of the city's posh restaurants . . . .

"What have you done this time for which I am expected, and do hereby forgive you?," exclaimed his delighted wife.

"Right!" he replied. "It's because you don't know anything about running a business and know it and I wouldn't have it any other way, and because I've become a male chauvinist and don't give a damn who knows that — so you be ready in time, you hear me?" □

DOLLARS VS. SENSE

For this bit of curiosa from life, the reader will have to provide your own punch line — if there is one:

It had been a hectic day on the phone, with one call following right on top of another. From my Market Street office on the third floor of the building, I could look down on one of San Francisco's busiest street corners. Taking a few minutes break, I got up to stretch. Idly gazing through the window, I could see a crowd forming about the entry to a large variety store. People were gathering around the figure of a man lying stretched out flat on his back, the blood drained from his face, his appearance lifeless. He didn't look drunk. A diabetic, drugged or an epileptic fit, perhaps. I guessed he would be in his twenties. He was wearing a brown sweater and slacks, his shoes well shined.

Again my phone rang. This time it was a wrong number. I returned to the window. In those few moments, several dollars in coins had been tossed down to the unconscious man. I saw a greenback floating down over his body. A lone, middle-aged little woman wearing a long coat, was determinedly working her way through the crowd. As she approached the man, she took off the coat. Squatting at his side and disregarding the scattering money, she struggled to push the coat under the supine figure, while the people surrounding them gaped. I recalled having read that when a person is in a state of shock, the first sensible thing to do is to take steps to keep the victim warm.

About that time, the police officer normally on traffic duty at that corner had made his way to the scene and to the man's side. Between him and the lady, the man was wrapped in her coat. My phone rang; it turned out to be a prolonged conversation. When I finally got back to the window to look again, the man was gone, the crowd had dispersed and an ambulance was just pulling away from the curb.   ☐

FABLE OF THE BEE AND THE BULL

The feud of hate between the bumble bee and the bull had been going on for a long time. One hot summer day, while browsing in the fields, the bull happened upon the bee who was dozing on a leaf of clover. With one big chomp of his great jaws, the bull gulped the bee down.

When the bee awoke he found himself in the deep, dark caverns of the bull's stomach. "Oh, boy!" he exulted. "What a break! How did I ever get such a wonderful opportunity! Wow! Will I sting this bull — but good!" though chuckling gleefully over the anticipated attack, he realized that it had been, indeed, an awfully warm, sleep-inducing day. He still felt drowsy. "I think," he ruminated, "I'll just have myself a little nap first. Then, when I awake, I'll be all refreshed, my stinger will be good and strong, and will I give it to this bull — and how!" So he curled up and soon fell asleep.

But when he awoke — the bull was gone!

MORAL: Do it now! □

A GREAT LIFE

His was the luxurious existence of the wealthy. None of the struggles for this one with living expenses, the rent or mortgage payments, the high cost of food, of doctor's bills, of rising taxes, of inflation and, of course, he had no worries about the proper carrying out of the housekeeping chores in his air-conditioned home, so comfortably warmed in winter and pleasantly cool in summer.

When he awoke in the morning, he would yawn and stretch himself into wakefulness. It was his habit to amble out through the garden, stroll down the street, sometimes stopping to exchange amenities with other early rising friends. After a while, his appetite now well stimulated, he would return home where a nutritious meal had been prepared for him, the food selected to conform with his allergies and his tastes. After eating, still feeling a bit languid perhaps, he might stretch out and snooze for a bit, later to pass the day as fancy prompted.

An enviable life — one to dream about, eh?

So why is it, when somebody tries to describe how hard, how tough, how miserable things are with him, he says he is "leading a dog's life"? □

UH — MIND IF I SMOKE?

Like most veteran smokers, I was not only bored stiff but highly resentful when some well-meaning non-smoker made me the objective in recounting what cigarettes did to one's health — especially annoying when it came from some self-righteous do gooder who had recently quit. So many times, I had heard, read and yawned through it all. I could recite just about as well as a doctor the various forms of lung ailments, the heart disease and all the whatever dread evils of smoking.

In consequence, now that I no longer smoke, I am not going to inflict myself on others with any gloomy preaching. Absolutely no "reformed drunkard" act! The only reason I bring the subject up here is because, in the interval that has passed since I smoked my last cigarette, I have had revealed to me a couple of conditions that, with all the brouhaha about the evils of smoking, strangely enough just never got my attention. What I mean is:

The smoker doesn't realize he carries with him a *smell* offensive to the non-smoker which, to some degree, makes his *presence* seriously disagreeable. Great thing for a rep, eh — trying to make a good impression? It is a circumstance of which I was unaware when I was smoking. In fact, I particularly prided myself on my smoking manners. For example, I never reached for a cigarette without offering to share my pack. If it was refused, I always asked the other fellow if he minded my smoking, taking his shrugging, "Sure, go ahead" for granted.

It's not only the smoker's body or clothes that exhude offensive odors. When I get into an auto now whose occupant has been smoking, the atmosphere of stale smoke assails my nostrils; it can take quite a while before I am able to disregard its unpleasantness. Something of the same stink strikes me upon entering a room where so many things like uphol- stery and draperies retain smoke odors. A non-smoking friend of mine was telling me that when his wife has been at the beauty parlor, though she herself didn't smoke, he could smell smoke in her hair, a stale residue left by the operator who smoked while working on her.

I wasn't aware that when I expelled a cloud of smoke, the other fellow might momentarily hold his breath or tactfully turn his head away. Being entirely accustomed to re-breath- ing my exhalations and, if I were calling on a customer, being engrossed in my sales talk, I would have no realization I was making the other fellow uncomfortable. Now I wonder how often some of my most telling points went up in smoke, so to speak, because I was unconsciously causing distraction in my prospect's mind!

There's more to this that meets the nose, such as creating disturbing fumes for people who never started smoking at all, whose senses have not been impaired by drawing those un- natural vapors into their lungs. Then, too, you have people with lung or heart conditions that didn't necessarily originate in smoking but who are allergic to it. Perhaps most important of all to consider are those who recently quit. Though toler- antly inviting you to go ahead and smoke if you wish, it follows that, as every smoker knows, when one starts up, the other is impelled to follow suit — and the quitter doesn't love you for putting temptation in his way!

No, sir — don't let those non-smokers tell you they "don't mind" your smoking! The hell they don't! But unfortunate- ly, believing it useless or thinking to be considerate, *most* non-smokers *don't* tell you smoking bothers them — though they keep thinking they wish you wouldn't and they can hardly wait for you to get the hell out. Considering all a rep has to go through to make himself *welcome* by the trade — ! It's an aspect for a smoking rep to think about — namely, the effect on his sales presentation if he is making the prospective customer uncomfortable.

Well — like I promised — no preaching about the evils of smoking. Just making conversation — thought I'd mention it. How's things out your way? ☐

IDEALS AND MAKING MONEY — HAH!

People beyond count have made inestimable amounts of money out of the great mechanical, scientific and technological developments of modern times. At the same time, we have among us those idealistic youths who, in ringing rhetoric, decry the waste of human energy given over to the mundane occupation of making money, while engaged in thumbing their way through the world. Well — don't sell the hitch-hikers short, despite their devotion to a life style defying what we elders refer to as "the laws of economics." In fact, in all probability, among those young people there may be one, still unknown, perhaps extremely gifted, who is preoccupied with developing a method of continued existence without money and, you know what? Once he has perfected his idea and brought it into use, I'll bet he makes a fortune out of it!

That the best things in life are free makes a pleasant, fetching song but those of us who have had to traverse the hard, rocky road between dreams and reality, who have lived from the end of the horse-and-buggy period to the dawn of intriguing inter-planet travel, learned long ago the necessity for devoting the better part of our days to making money.

While my ten-year-old grandson watched fearfully, I mounted his beloved bicycle — myself doubtful, wondering if I still retained enough boyhood ability to handle the contraption. After a few wobbly moments, I was elated to find I could propel the bike in a fairly straight line. Throwing dignity to the winds, I continued riding (but cau-

tiously, on the sidewalk!) around the block.

The years rolled back. As though the subject of a movie flashback, I seemed to be delivering newspapers, turning into driveways and ringing doorbells, soliciting subscriptions to the "Saturday Evening Post" and the "Ladies Home Journal," or bringing magazines to those kindly neighbors and family friends who had already succumbed to the little redheaded salesman's timorous sales pitch by previously subscribing.

The scene dissolved; the bicycle changed to an automobile, the driveways to parking lots of nationally known electronic manufacturers, with whose purchasing departments I was negotiating orders for products to be incorporated in equipment destined to soon land on the moon.

Fade out.

I returned the precious bike intact, to the youngster's undisguised relief and he rode off, to leave me speculating on the changes wrought in working one's way through life by means of the bicycle to automobile and even to the aeroplane. Something about using the thumb for transportation seemed to be out of joint, so to speak. I try to understand but I find it difficult to justify the paradox of denouncing material aims with the critic's unabashed thumb proclaiming his desire to utilize the results of the despised materialism.

Which is by way of emphasizing, admittedly, that this book is dedicated to helping those burdened with the problems of acquiring the means needed to pay the doctors for delivering and tending in illness those very same critics, for building and equipping the schools and colleges they attend, for supplying the food, the shelter, the clothes, and all those other things which Mother Nature doesn't provide or that otherwise don't come out of nowhere for free but which, somehow, continue to prove necessary for people's existence.

In short — this book is pointedly for those who have attained a reasonable degree of maturity. It was written for the man who believes in and always tries to retain the ideals of his own youth, who may very well assert, plaintively or stoutly perhaps, he sees nothing so bad about trying to become a *rich* idealist. And to all such — good luck, friends! □

— F.L.